GUIDANCE MONOGRAPH SERIES

SHELLEY C. STONE

BRUCE SHERTZER

Editors

GUIDANCE MONOGRAPH SERIES

The general purpose of Houghton Mifflin's Guidance Monograph Series is to provide high quality coverage of topics which are of abiding importance in contemporary counseling and guidance practice. In a rapidly expanding field of endeavor, change and innovation are inevitably present. A trend accompanying such growth is greater and greater specialization. Specialization results in an increased demand for materials which reflect current modifications in guidance practice while simultaneously treating the field in greater depth and detail than commonly found in textbooks and brief journal articles.

The list of eminent contributors to this series assures the reader expert treatment of the areas covered. The monographs are designed for consumers with varying familiarity to the counseling and guidance field. The editors believe that the series will be useful to experienced practitioners as well as beginning students. While these groups may use the monographs with somewhat different goals in mind, both will benefit from the treatment given to content areas.

The content areas treated have been selected because of specific criteria. Among them are timeliness, practicality, and persistency of the issues involved. Above all, the editors have attempted to select topics which are of major substantive concern to counseling and guidance personnel.

Shelley C. Stone

Bruce Shertzer

TRANSACTIONAL
ANALYSIS
APPROACH TO
COUNSELING

A. LOREAN ROBERTS

THE UNIVERSITY OF TOLEDO

HOUGHTON MIFFLIN COMPANY · BOSTON

ATLANTA · DALLAS · GENEVA, ILL. · HOPEWELL, N.J. · PALO ALTO

ISBN: 0–395–200350

Library of Congress Catalog Card
Number: 74–11960

CONTENTS

LIST OF FIGURES

EDITORS' INTRODUCTION

Since the mid-1960s, Transactional Analysis, as a method for the amelioration and understanding of psychological interactions and problems, has grown tremendously in popularity. The publication in 1964 of Eric Berne's *Games People Play* followed in 1967 by Thomas Harris' *I'm OK — You're OK* contributed immeasurably to the public interest and awareness of transactional analysis. While its basis is to be found in several well-respected and accepted theories of personality and treatment, the theory, method, and application of transactional analysis have gained great currency with many professionals and the public because, compared to its precursors, it is relatively simple, straightforward, and understandable.

Lorean Roberts has done an excellent job in presenting transactional analysis in a highly readable fashion. Her presentation is both thorough and knowledgeable. It is replete with examples and applications for use with students in the school setting at all grade levels, and for use with the adults (parents, teachers and others) who play highly important roles in the lives of children of all ages. This monograph deserves reading and rereading. It will stimulate additional interest in the sources upon which it is based as well as thoughtful consideration of its usefulness to and application by counselors and teachers.

SHELLEY C. STONE
BRUCE SHERTZER

AUTHOR'S INTRODUCTION

One of the recurring difficulties that seems to be experienced by many counselors is that of translating theory into practice. Counselors-in-training frequently complain that the terminology of counseling theories is confusing and the related personality constructs are not easily understood. Furthermore, the theoretical explanations of how behaviors are acquired and subsequently changed represent too many viable, yet often conflicting, alternatives for action. It is not uncommon, therefore, that counselors enter into practice in the schools without having clarified and internalized a theoretical point of view out of which to operate. This results in confusion and frustration for the counselor as he finds himself not knowing how to deal with certain situations that arise, or how to proceed with counselees that present serious personal concerns. The problem for the counselor seems to be that theory is difficult to relate directly to reality and experience.

The transactional analysis approach to counseling, though not offered as a panacea, helps bridge the gaps between theory and practice. The terminology is straightforward and familiar. The approach and its related personality theory are easily understood because their components are recognizable and observable in one's own behavior as well as in day to day contacts with others. Since the theory is based on reality and is constantly being affirmed through observable behaviors, it provides a concrete basis for behavior change; and change itself is easily perceived by both counselor and counselee.

This monograph presents the theoretical bases for transactional analysis in a brief, yet hopefully understandable, form. Examples related to everyday life have been included for the purpose of clarification as well as to reinforce the point that this is a theory one *lives*. The intent of the theoretical presentation is to provide a basic framework for understanding the practical usefulness of the approach. In addition, it is hoped that it will stimulate the interest of the readers sufficiently that they will be enticed to further their knowledge of TA by reading the works of Berne and Harris.

The section devoted to the application of transactional analysis in the schools is intended to demonstrate through example the practicability of the approach. Furthermore, this section illustrates how counselees can become active participants in the process of changing their behavior, and how they are able to gain an understanding of the dynamics of their own and others' personalities. The many ways in which transactional analysis can be implemented in individual and group counseling as well as in the classroom have been merely touched upon. The involved counselor will find countless situations in which TA has a place.

A. LOREAN ROBERTS

1

An Overview of
Transactional Analysis

Transactional Analysis is an ego system of psychotherapy which was developed by Eric Berne. Growing out of his experience and practice in orthodox psychoanalysis, the theory retains some elements of psychoanalysis, as well as concepts from social and individual psychology, and learning theory. Indigenous to groups, this approach to psychotherapy focuses upon the reality-based components of the personality: ego states, the involvement of those elements in the course of social transactions, and the manner in which the ego state transaction interrelationship determines individual need satisfaction and the pursuit of life goals.

Berne (1961) states that,

> Structural and transactional analysis offer a systematic, consistent theory of personality and social dynamics derived from clinical experience, and an actionistic, rational form of therapy which is suitable for, easily understood by, and naturally adapted to the great majority of psychiatric patients. [p. 21]

Berne further declares that transactional analysis overcomes the difficulties encountered in other psychotherapies, i.e., the neglect of archaic feelings which influence behavior in "parental" approaches, and the possibility of delay in establishing inner controls of behavior in "rational" therapies. Both of these problems are met in transactional analysis by providing the patient with the tools to establish controls from within at an early stage in therapy, as well as by the fact that the therapist maintains an awareness of the archaic elements within the personality. The tools include an understanding of one's ego states and the manner in which they are expressed, and a simple but useful vocabulary to describe the dynamics of personal behavior.

One of the outstanding and attractive characteristics of transactional analysis is, in fact, its simplicity. Although the theory itself is complex, patients and laymen are able to understand and use transactional analysis with relative ease; and the use of technical psychological terminology to describe or explain phenomena is minimized. Six common words form the basic vocabulary: Parent, Adult, Child, pastimes, games, and script.

Two kinds of analyses are fundamental to transactional analysis: structural analysis and transactional analysis. Structural analysis involves the analysis and recognition of the individual's ego states: the Parent, the Adult, and the Child (P-A-C)[1]. Transactional analysis, a term which serves the dual function of referring to the total theoretical approach as well as to an integral part of the theory, refers here to the analysis of a single social unit of action (transaction) based on the ego states involved. Pastimes and games are larger units of social action. Pastimes refer to socially prescribed and accepted ways of structuring one's "free" time. Games refer to psychologically rewarding transactions based on ulterior motives. Game analysis and script analysis are two other fundamental components of transactional analysis. The understanding and usefulness of these two types of analysis are dependent upon sound instruction in structural and transactional analysis. Game analysis involves roles, social and psychological messages sent concurrently, ego states, and a denouement, colloquially called a payoff. Script analysis is concerned with attempting to determine the nature of one's life drama.

Although transactional analysis has been criticized for its oversimplification, especially in reference to its language, the fact that it is easily understood and quickly related to personal relationships, accounts for a large part of the increasing popularity of the approach.

[1] In keeping with transactional analysis literature, it is important to note that parent, adult, and child written in small letters refer to actual people, whereas, Parent, Adult, and Child refer to ego states. These three words, with their differentiating capital or small initial letters, will be used consistently throughout the text.

History and Development

Important Individuals

Eric Berne (1910–1970) was born Eric Lennard Bernstein, the son of a general medical practitioner in Montreal. Berne's mother was a writer, and both of his parents graduated from McGill University where Berne was later to receive his medical degrees. He received his B.A. in 1931, and his M.D. and C.M. (Master of Surgery) in 1935.

Moving from Canada to the United States to serve his internship, Berne began a residency in psychiatry in the Psychiatric Clinic of the Yale University School of Medicine in 1936. In 1941 he was appointed to Mt. Zion Hospital in New York City as Clinical Assistant in Psychiatry. Prior to his appointment at Mt. Zion, Berne became a United States citizen and changed his name officially to Eric Berne. Also during this time, he established private practices in Norwalk, Connecticut, and New York City; met his first wife by whom he had two children; and began training at the New York Psychoanalytic Institute. In 1943, Berne entered the Army Medical Corps, serving as an officer until 1946. During the last two years of his military career, he began working with civilian therapy groups while stationed in Utah.

In 1946, upon his discharge from the service, Berne moved to California and resumed his training in psychoanalysis at the San Francisco Psychoanalytic Institute, where he worked with Erik Erikson. This same year he published *The Mind in Action* which has been revised and is now published under the title, *A Layman's Guide to Psychiatry and Psychoanalysis* (1968). Shortly thereafter, Berne met and fell in love with his second wife, whom he married in 1949. This marriage produced two more children, both sons. In 1964, the marriage ended in a friendly divorce. It was between the years 1949 and 1964 that the major portion of Berne's writing was done.

In the early 1950's, Berne was busy with three professional appointments: Assistant Psychiatrist at Mt. Zion Hospital in San Francisco; Consultant to the Surgeon General of the U.S. Army; and Adjunct and Attending Psychiatrist at the Veterans Administration Mental Hygiene Clinic in San Francisco. During this same period he also conducted private practices in both Carmel and San Francisco. In 1951, Berne started a clinical seminar in his home in San Francisco. Later in 1958, it became the San Francisco Social Psychiatry Seminars, Inc., and published in January of 1962 the first *Transactional Analysis Bulletin*, with Berne as editor.

In 1967, Berne was married a third time and was divorced in 1970. During this time Berne was deeply involved in writing commitments, and shortly before his death in July of 1970, he had completed two books, *Sex in Human Loving* (1970), and *What Do You Say After You Say Hello?* (1972). In addition to his widely read *Games People Play* (1964), and the books previously mentioned, Berne has authored *Transactional Analysis in Psychotherapy* (1961), *The Structure and Dynamics of Organizations and Groups* (1963), *Principles of Group Treatment* (1966), and *The Happy Valley* (1968), as well as numerous journal articles.

Another individual who has contributed significantly to the growth of the transactional analysis movement is Thomas A. Harris, M.D., author of the bestselling *I'm OK — You're OK: A Practical Guide to Transactional Analysis* (1967). Harris was born in Texas, and received his B.S. degree from the University of Arkansas Medical School in 1938, and his M.D. in 1940 from Temple University Medical School. After his psychiatric residency at St. Elizabeth's Hospital in Washington, D.C., Harris served as Chief of the Psychiatric Service at the Philadelphia Naval Hospital, Chief of the Psychiatric Branch of the Bureau of Medicine and Surgery in the Navy Department, associate professor of psychiatry at the University of Arkansas School of Medicine, and Director of the Department of Institutions in the state of Washington. In 1956 he entered private practice in Sacramento, and has served as director, trustee, and vice president of the International Transactional Analysis Association. Harris studied under Berne as well as Harry Stack Sullivan and Frieda Fromm-Reichmann.

The Origins

The origins of transactional analysis may be traced to a series of articles on intuition written by Berne from 1949 to 1962, although Berne had dealt with the subject first in a paper read in 1947 before the San Francisco and Los Angeles Psychoanalytic Societies. In the first paper (Berne, 1949) a basic definition of intuition was offered. He proposed that intuition was knowledge based on experience, acquired through sensory contact, but without awareness of the nature of its acquisition. He further noted that intuition could be facilitated or impaired by certain conditions, and that the intuitive mood could be improved with practice. The second paper (Berne, 1952) had to do with diagnostic categories. Observing the reactions of soldiers to doctors in an army separation center, Berne classified their behavior into three groups on the basis of facial expressions, gestures, voluntary and involuntary movements, and other observable behaviors. The attention given to stimulus and response in the context of individual psychology was later to become the heart of transactional analysis, and the types of behaviors observed later became useful in identifying ego states. Both of these papers dealt with the therapist as intuitor, and intuition was to become identified as a part of the Child ego state.

Berne's third paper (1953) spoke to the topic of the nature of communication. Drawing from the field of cybernetics, Berne compared two kinds of communication available from machines: "information," a precise message sent to the receiver; and "noise," extraneous messages reflecting the condition of the machine itself. Translating the two levels of messages to the field of psychology, Berne states that a precise message or "information" is impossible to communicate to another person.

> The value of communication (to the receiver) cannot be set by the communicant, but only by the receiver. No matter how anxious the communicant is to form a precise message, his communication cannot be limited to what he intends. Furthermore, the unintended communications, which from his view are "noise" are of more psychological value than the intended one. [p. 190]

Focusing on the "noise" of communication, Berne further stated,

> In the case of interpersonal relationships, in general, intended, precise, formal, rational, verbal communications are of less value than inadvertent, ambiguous, informal, nonrational, nonverbal communication. [p. 190]

"Noise" was termed latent communication, and "information" was considered manifest communication. Berne believed that both were sent frequently, and that the effect was the arousal of a latent response in the receiver which was of importance to both parties. Later Berne translated this concept of dual levels of communication into ulterior transactions, the basis of psychological games (Dusay, 1971).

Berne first used structural analysis as a part of his therapeutic approach in 1954 (Berne, 1961). During the next two years the principles of transactional and game analysis were clarified and systematically researched. During this time another important piece was added to the evolving theory which Berne referred to as primal images (Berne, 1957b). By thorough research and observations of the first transactional analysis group he found that persons had vivid, extraordinarily accurate images of childhood happenings which affected the manner in which they related to people in later life. He believed there was a triad — primal images, primal judgments, and reactions to people — which was influential in an individual's behavior and goal seeking; and he found that the images were primarily sexual or about sexual organs. These images caused individuals to make judgments about others and, on the basis of the judgments, to avoid or approach them. This particular discovery would later be crucial to the identification of the Child ego state and to the unconscious moves individuals make in playing games and in fulfilling their life script.

Continuing his research, Berne presented evidence that ego states are conscious parts of the personality, and that more than one ego state can obviously exist within an individual (Berne, 1957a). Although Berne had not yet broken with formal psychoanalysis and believed that the conscious and unconscious, the id and the ego, were involved in the dynamics of the phenomena, this was not of primary importance: what was important was that patient and therapist both were aware of an observable difference in functioning and thinking on the part of the patient, i.e., the observance of two distinct ego states. During 1957 and 1958, papers read to the Western Regional Meeting of the American Group Psychotherapy Association in Los Angeles, and later published in the *American Journal of Psychotherapy,* outlined Berne's method of diagnosis and treatment, the concepts of P-A-C, structural analysis and ego states, games, and scripts (Cheney, 1971). Formally breaking with psychoanalysis at this time, Berne still embraced the psychoanalytic theory of personality and incorporated psychoanalysis into his therapy process. The point of departure with Freudian psychoanalysis comes in regard to ego states, which Berne sees not as concepts but as phenomenological realities, dynamic in themselves rather than reflections of the unconscious.

Struggle Against Criticism

Shapiro (1969) sees transactional analysis as a comparatively complete theory of personality and psychotherapeutic technology, and states that the identification of ego states and the analysis of transactions are the major contributions of Berne. Furthermore, he views transactional analysis as heuristic and functional, and the concepts of the theory as utilitarian. On the other hand, Shapiro has reservations regarding the emphasis on deficiency motivation based on the drives of sex and aggression. He finds the theory lacking in reference to curiosity, growth, or other drives which are characteristic of what Maslow (1954) refers to as "b" motivation, or growth. Evaluating Berne's theory as deterministic, Shapiro believes that this position allows little opportunity for creativity and emergent behavior.

Responding to this criticism, Berne (1969) refutes the notion of a negative emphasis. He suggests that the criticism may be a reaction to this more direct and different approach to therapy. Berne states in reference to patients,

> If I can scrape the barnacles and blisters off his personality, he will be able to sail much more quickly and smoothly to wherever he wants to go, and I have full confidence that the evolutionary force of *Phusis* will direct him to some worthwhile way of life if I just leave him alone and don't nag him after I have fulfilled my part of the contract. If he still needs a guru, then I haven't done that properly. [p. 278]

During the time that Berne was formulating the ideas of transactional analysis, he was testing them in the seminars which he had been conducting weekly in Monterey. In the early fifties he also began a weekly seminar in his home which was to become the San Francisco Social Psychiatry Seminars, Inc., mentioned above as the first official organization for transactional analysis. Chartered in 1960, the non-profit educational organization published the first issue of the *Transactional Analysis Bulletin* in 1962, with Berne as the editor. By the following year, membership in the Seminars had grown in California and there were members in 12 other states as well (Berne, 1968a). In 1964 members represented 24 states, Canada, Costa Rica and England, and the San Francisco Social Psychiatry Seminars, Inc., became the International Transactional Analysis Association. In January of 1971, the official publication of the ITAA was changed from the *Transactional Analysis Bulletin* to the *Transactional Analysis Journal*. The first issue of the newly named journal was a memorial to Eric Berne who had died in July of the preceding year. Currently, there are more than 3,700 members in ITAA representing several countries. The organization is in the process of forming an ITAA college or university for the purposes of maintaining and extending training and education of practitioners (Everts, 1973).

Much of Berne's professional life was spent struggling to attain the title "psychoanalyst" and at the same time attempting to improve psychoanalysis, according to Cheney (1971). Following two years of training at the New York Psychoanalytic Institute and another 10 years at the San Francisco Psychoanalytic Institute, Berne was denied membership in 1956 in the latter institute on the grounds that he was not ready and needed more training. This incident provided the impetus for developing a new approach to psychoanalysis and before the end of the year Berne had written two papers on intuition, the beginnings of his theory. Even after his theory was developed and tested, he gained little acceptance from fellow psychiatrists who resisted the newness and simplicity of transactional analysis. A few months prior to his death, however, Berne read a paper before the American Psychiatric Association Annual in San Francisco to a large audience. Cheney reports,

> Despite an ample question and answer period, there was not one remark emanating from the listeners which was hostile, tinged with ridicule or skepticism. Any fair-minded observer who was present would have had to say that TA was being taken with utter seriousness, indeed, the perceptive witness would have had to report TA had won real recognition as an important new psychotherapy and was no longer capable of being ignored. [p. 21]

2

General Principles
of Transactional Analysis

The underlying principles of Transactional Analysis are best understood when explored in relation to the four analytic components of the theory:

Structural analysis: the analysis of the ego states manifest in the individual personality

Transactional analysis: the analysis of interpersonal interactions and communications

Games: transactions initiated with ulterior motives and which culminate in a psychological "pay off"

Scripts: analogous to a theatrical play, the way in which one unconsciously plays out his life drama

Structural Analysis

Ego States

Berne (1963) defines ego states as a coherent system of feelings with its related set of behavior patterns. Each person possesses three ego states: the Parent, the Adult, and the Child. Particular behaviors, gestures, facial expressions, vocabularies, and voices are associated with each (Berne, 1961). The Parent is the keeper of beliefs, values, and attitudes, and operates under the principle of delayed gratification. The Adult functions in a computer-like mode, realistically taking in and assessing available data and making decisions objectively. The Child consists of emotions and feelings, is both fun-loving and destructive, and is primarily concerned with the immediate gratification of needs. Ego states constitute separate entities, and it is possible to determine which ego state is operating or "in charge" at any given moment by observing an individual's verbal and nonverbal behavior. One of the hallmarks of transactional analysis is the graphic representation of the ego states and the P-A-C structure (Figure 1).

Clinical observation of the phenomenon of changing personal demeanor led Berne and his colleagues to hypothesize that the human brain functions much like a tape recorder — recording words, gestures, feelings, and responses exactly as they are perceived by an individual from the moment of birth on — and that replays of any previously experienced situation, along with the emotions that accompanied the experience, are available for reliving when certain external stimuli evoke recollection of the experience. Support for this position was found in the work of Penfield (1952) who discovered that direct electrode stimulation of the temporal lobes of the brain evoked not only precise memories of a past event, but also the emotions that were present at the time — in other words, the complete ego state could be recalled. Furthermore, it was demonstrated that the person could, under the conditions of electrode stimulation, be both observer and participant in the recollection, thus establishing that two ego states could be in operation at any given time and that they are distinct and separate from each other.

Penfield's findings and the clinical data collected provide the evidence necessary to substantiate a crucial principle in Transactional Analysis: that ego states are phenomenological realities and not psychological concepts such as Freud's superego, ego, and id. As Berne (1966, p. 35) states, "[Freud's] Superego, Ego, and Id are constructs, while Parent, Adult, and Child represent real people whose names and addresses are on civil record." The Parent exists as such because of input collected from actual interactions with one's parents and/or other authority figures; the Child is a collection of all experiences that occurred when one was, in fact, a child; and the Adult, which becomes functional at about age 12 (English, 1973), holds autonomous modes of behaving and responding which

FIGURE 1
The P-A-C Model and Corresponding Ego State Structures

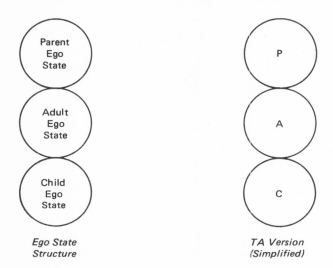

Ego State
Structure

TA Version
(Simplified)

develop as one checks out Parent and Child messages with reality.

As Berne (1961) notes, ego states denote states of mind and their related patterns of behavior. Each ego state has its corresponding psychic organ: the *exteropsyche* (Parent, identicatory), the *neopsyche* (Adult, data-processing), and the *archaeopsyche* (Child, repressive). The theoretical basis for structural analysis incorporates the psychic organs and the previously stated facts concerning one's life experiences: The Child is comprised of relics of childhood which survive as a complete ego state (archaeopsychic relics); the Adult, as a tester of reality, with reality-testing a function of an ego state, not an isolated "capacity" (neopsychic functioning); and the Parent demonstrates that an outside individual can take over a complete ego state if the messages that have been recorded are so powerful that the person functions in much the same manner as the outside individual when the Parent has the executive power (exteropsychic functioning).

The Parent

The Parent ego state is a set of feelings, attitudes, and behavior patterns which resemble those of a parental figure (Berne, 1961). It is a collection of externally imposed events recorded primarily during the first five years of life. The messages include both verbal and nonverbal communications from and between parents, and are recorded literally and precisely for the child is unable to comprehend any extenuating circumstances, i.e., illness, drunkeness, anxiety, and the like, which might qualify what is being perceived. The primary Parenting agents are the individual's parents; however, similar kinds of input are added later from the school and the church. The Parenting messages stress duty, responsibility, how to behave to gain approval, and include statements about prejudices, attitudes, and values. The vocabulary of the Parent includes such words as, "should," "ought," "must," "have to," and similar directives. The underlying communication from Parenting agents is, "Control your Child, and delay gratification."

The Parent has no fun, but that should not be construed as meaning that the Parent is totally stern, restrictive, or oppressive. Since there are two kinds of Parenting messages, critical or controlling and nurturing, there are also two kinds of behaviors being recorded in the Parent. The critical Parent admonishes, punishes, frowns, rejects, and elicits feelings of discomfort, anxiety, defensiveness, and worthlessness in the Child; the nurturing Parent comforts, soothes, praises, and provides the stability that allows the Child to be spontaneous, creative, kind and considerate. The function of the Parent is to provide a set of values and standards for behavior for the individual and, therefore, to conserve energy and diminish anxiety.

The Adult

The Adult ego state is "characterized by an autonomous set of feelings, attitudes, and behavior patterns which are adapted to the current reality," (Berne, 1961, p. 76). It is not controlled by Parent restrictions, nor is it at the mercy of Child emotions. It does, however, receive and consider messages from both, assesses those data against reality, and makes decisions on the basis of "truth." For example, a young person has left his bicycle unlocked and unattended while he makes a small purchase. His Parent recalls that he should not leave his belongings where others might have the opportunity to steal them; but his Child insists that he won't be gone long, and that there isn't time to waste taking care of his bicycle. Upon returning and finding his bicycle missing, his Adult may well decide that this bit of Parent advice is useful and should be retained. Similarly, one's Child may react in a hurt and pouting way when events do not go as anticipated. The Adult may reason that the situation does not reflect a personal blow, but that unexpected and unavoidable circumstances have arisen. This reality does not justify the child-like reaction of the Child ego state, and the Adult will take charge and make the best of the situation. The ultimate function of the Adult is to deal with presenting situations in an organized, adaptable, and intelligent way — in other words, reality testing. The Adult exists intact in each individual regardless of his personal limitations such as intelligence or disabilities, or cultural limitations such as race, ethnic or socioeconomic background. This is an important assumption of the theory for it implies that the approach has wide application and is not limited to a specific population.

The Child

Berne (1961) defines the child as a set of feelings, attitudes, and behavior patterns which are relics of the individual's own childhood. The Child is most likely to emerge in response to a communication from a Parent ego state. As with the Parent, the Child exhibits two forms of functioning: the Natural Child and the Adapted Child. The Natural Child strives for total freedom, to do what it wants to do when it wants to do it. It has natural impulses for love, affection, creativity, aggression, and rebellion, and it acts spontaneously. The Adapted Child, on the other hand, is influenced by the Parent and it has discovered ways, usually compliance, avoidance, or procrastination, to deal with feelings in a manner which will not bring forth Parental reprimand. The Adapted Child duplicates the original reactions the individual had toward his parents during childhood, and holds feelings such as guilt, fright, sullenness, confusion, and other childlike emotions. The emerging Adult in the Child is called the Little Professor. This part of the Child ego state is the source of intuition, creativity, manipulation, and has the ability to act as negotiator between the Natural Child and the Adapted Child. The Child has the capacity for both constructive and destructive behavior in its constant struggle for expression and immediate gratification.

Every person has the capacity for a fully functioning Parent, Adult, and Child. It may be, however, that one particular ego state is more powerful than the others and therefore does not allow the other ego states full expression, or that an ego state is not sufficiently strengthened through use to gain executive power. Circumstances which influence the ability of an ego state to emerge include the forces acting on each of the ego states at any given time, the permeability of the boundaries between the ego states, and the cathectic capacity of each of them (Berne, 1961). It may be, too, that an ego state is contaminated, fixed, or decommissioned, conditions which will be discussed later.

Given the capacity for three fully functioning ego states, it is assumed that the psychologically healthy individual can activate any one of the states appropriately and at will. Cathexis, or flow of psychic energy, from one ego state to another accounts for the expression of the Parent, the Adult, or the Child. The ego state that is most highly cathected will be the one that is exhibited. Berne (1961) discusses three types of cathexis: bound, unbound, and free. Bound cathexis is potential psychic energy; unbound cathexis is psychic energy in motion, or kinetic energy; and free cathexis is energy activated by choice. How these kinds of cathexis combine accounts not only for the ability of an ego state to gain control but also for how one perceives his "real Self."

It has been established that ego states can be experienced as separate entities and that it is possible to diagnose which ego state has the executive or controlling power by observing an individual's overt behavior. This suggests some sort of boundaries between the ego states. Also, clinical observation and case histories indicate that patients experience the different ego states as their "real Self" or not their "real Self" (Berne, 1961). These two conditions, expression of an ego state and experiencing the "real Self," may be explained by the flow of the different kinds of cathexis between ego states. Bound and unbound cathexis are unable to permeate the boundaries of the ego states; however, free cathexis can flow from one to another. When unbound and free cathexes are combined, the result is active cathexis. The ego state which has the greatest amount of active cathexis (unbound plus free) is the one which has the executive power. The ego state which contains the greatest amount of free cathexis is perceived as the "real Self" even though it may not have executive power at the time (pp. 40–41).

In the case in which an individual has a weakly cathected Adult, the behavior he exhibits may be considered by some as "immature." In transactional analysis, however, it is believed that every person has a complete Adult fully capable of functioning given the opportunity for expression and practice. For this reason the words "mature" and "immature" are excluded from the transactional analysis vocabulary. There can be no such thing as an "immature" person for the potential for a strong Adult is always there. It may be that the behavior exhibited may seem immature, but it is more of an indication that the Child is in command. In addition, the word "childish" is not used in transactional analysis. Behavior may be child-like, i.e., reminiscent of a child, but not childish for that too implies immaturity. If the Child ego state has the executive power, the behavior will of necessity be child-like.

The preceding discussion has focused primarily on first order structural analysis. Second order structural analysis is concerned with the substructures of the individual ego states. An example would be the substructures of the Parent. Not only is there the Critical Parent and the Nurturing Parent, but also finer delineations since the Parenting messages also incorporate parts of the Parenting agent's Parent, Adult, and Child. Second order structural analysis is most useful in script analysis.

Structural analysis is the prerequisite for transactional analysis for it enables the individual to understand the internal dialogues and the struggles between real parts of his personality. Furthermore, structural analysis allows the individual to identify which of his ego states is in power at any given time so that he may use that information to understand the nature of his behavior and the behavior of others within a social context: transactional analysis.

Transactional Analysis

Transactions are units of social action (Berne, 1963). When one person encounters another person and speaks, this is called the *transactional stimulus;* the ensuing reply is called the *transactional response* (Berne, 1964a). Transactional analysis is concerned with diagnosing the ego states from which the interchange is emanating for both persons involved, and clarifying the exchange. Transactions range from simple to highly complex: Berne (1972) states that there are nine complementary, 72 crossed, 6480 duplex, and 36 angular types possible (p. 20). Only the categories of transactions will be discussed here.

Complementary transactions occur when both parties speak from their Adults, or when the vectors are parallel as when Parent speaks to Child, and Child responds to Parent (Figure 2). Complementary transactions consist of exchanges in which response expectations are met and, therefore, can go on indefinitely so long as this condition (parallel vectors) exists.

Crossed transactions occur when the vectors are not parallel, and the result is discontinued communication. The most common type of crossed transaction results from Adult-Adult stimulus with a Parent-Child or Child-Parent response (Figure 3). Crossed transactions usually end in a deadlock unless the respondent is able to mobilize his Adult to complement the Adult in the other party; otherwise, the transaction is finished with one or both parties left silent, angry, or feeling hurt and misunderstood.

FIGURE 2
Complementary Transactions

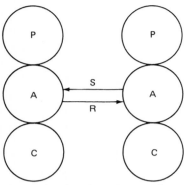 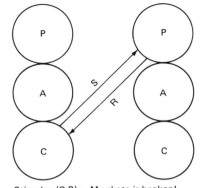

Stimulus (A-A): The roads are really slippery. I think I'll slow down.

Response (A-A): Yes, other drivers seem to have noticed that, too, for traffic has slowed considerably.

Stimulus (C-P): My skate is broken!

Response (P-C): Here, honey, let me see if I can fix it.

FIGURE 3
Crossed Transactions

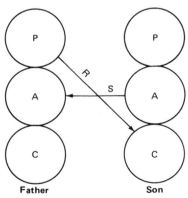 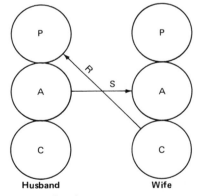

Father   Son   Husband   Wife

Stimulus (A-A): Dad, I got my home-work done in half the time I thought it would take.

Response (P-C): You surely weren't very careful then, son. You'd better check it for mistakes.

Stimulus (A-A): My secretary sure helped me out of a tight spot today.

Response (C-P): Maybe you'd like it better if she took care of all your problems.

Ulterior transactions involve more than two ego states in operation at the same time (Berne, 1964a). This type of transaction consists of one message being sent on a social level, usually Adult-Adult, and an implied message being sent on a psychological level in another ego state. Ulterior transactions occur in two types: angular (Figure 4) and duplex (Figure 5).

Ulterior transactions are the bases for games, one of the ways in which individuals structure time. Although time structuring will be treated more fully in the discussion of TA theory of personality, some mention of the concept of structured time seems appropriate at this time. Briefly, humans have a need for structuring or filling the time they have available for life (Berne, 1964a). They do this in several ways with the simplest being procedures and rituals. Procedures are Adult-Adult transactions focusing on reality as in the way people transact business, fulfill employment responsibilities, etc. Rituals are socially and culturally determined ways of behaving in certain settings, such as greeting rituals, leave-taking rituals, party rituals, and other informal but stereotyped ways of encountering people. Pastimes are more complex and semi-stereotyped time structuring devices, and usually occur in social situations during a waiting period. Berne (1964a) has labeled some popular pastimes as "PTA," "Ever Been," "General Motors," "Do You Know," "What Ever Became," and "Look Ma No Hands," to name but a few. The most complex way in which people structure time is to engage in games which are unconscious but purposeful, and which involve the manipulation of others in order to satisfy one's own psychological needs. Other ways to structure time are withdrawal and intimacy. Games serve to avoid intimacy which can come only through game-free, internally affective transactions.

Game Analysis

Berne (1967, p. 125) defines psychological games as "a recurring set of transactions, often repetitive, superficially rational, with a concealed motivation; or, more colloquially, as a series of transactions with a gimmick." As the definition indicates, games are a series of ulterior transactions which have complementary social transactions accompanied simultaneously by unverbalized complementary psychological transactions. Games have mottoes, colloquially called "sweatshirts," which identify the general play of the game, such as "Ain't It Awful," "Alcoholic," "Let's You and Him Fight," "Uproar," etc. Every game has a thesis (the general description of the game along with the social level sequence of events), an

FIGURE 4
Angular Ulterior Transactions

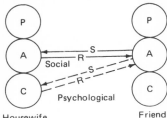

Housewife   Friend

Social level:
Stimulus (A-A): No more dessert for
me. It's too rich.

Response (A-A): Oh, I guess it is. I
won't have any more
right now either.

Psychological level:
Stimulus (A-C): No wonder you're so
fat.

Response (C-A): I'll show you I have
will power, but just
wait 'til you're gone.

FIGURE 5
Duplex Ulterior Transactions

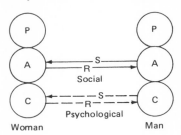

Woman   Man

Social level:
Stimulus (A-A): I know of a nice quiet
place where we can go
for a nightcap.

Response (A-A): Good, I'm in the mood
for soft lights and
good music.

Psychological level:
Stimulus (C-C): I'm going to make a
pass at you.

Response (C-C): I hope you make a pass
at me.

antithesis (the refusal to play or ways to stop the game), an aim (the general purpose of the game), roles for the players, and motivating psychological dynamics. The classification of games is based on the number of players, the currency used (words, money, body parts, etc.), clinical types, zonal factors (oral, anal, phallic), psycho-dynamic factors (projective, introjective, etc.), and instinctual factors. Other variables include the flexibility of the game with regard to the currency used, the tenacity one has for his game, and how intensely the game is played (Berne, 1964a). Game stages also are classified as First-Degree Games (socially acceptable), Second-Degree Games (no permanent damage to players but usu-ally concealed from public), and Third-Degree Games (played for keeps and usually with dramatic, often tragic outcomes) (Berne, 1964a).

One of the earliest games to be identified by Berne was "Why Don't You — Yes But" which is referred to as YDYB. The following is Berne's (1964a) analysis of this game. Thesis: See if you can present a solution I can't find fault with; Antithesis: "That is a difficult problem: what are you going to do about it?"; Aim: reas-surance; Roles: helpless person, advisors; Dynamics: surrender conflict (oral). The moves are (1) presentation of problem, solution offered; (2) solution objected to, another solution offered; and (3) another objection, disconsternation. On the social level the game paradigm is Adult-Adult:

> Adult: "What do you do if . . ."
> Adult: "Why don't you . . ."
> Adult: "Yes, but . . ."

Psychologically, the paradigm is Parent-Child:

> Parent: "I can make you grateful for my help."
> Child: "Go ahead and try."

Games related to YDYB are "Why Did You — No But," "Do Me Something," "Peasant," and "Stupid." The unsuspecting helper or advisor may get caught up in YDYB and play his own complemen-tary game, "I'm Only Trying to Help You," or ITHY, in which the helper keeps offering advice and solutions, the person asking for help keeps saying that the advice wasn't quite solving the situation, and so on. The "payoff" comes when the helpee bursts into the helper's office and exclaims, "Look what you made me do!" to which the helper says, "But I was only trying to help you." The helpee's payoff is that he has proved that no one can help him, and the helper's payoff is that he can't understand how people can be so ungrateful, especially when he has gone out of his way to be helpful.

Games may be depicted diagrammatically with the transactional P-A-C model, or with the game formula (Karpman, 1972):

$$C + G \rightarrow R \times S = P$$

which translates as ". . . Con plus Gimmick gives the Response; then there's the Switch that gives the Payoff [p. 140]." The Con is the initial trick of the game, the Gimmick is the other person's weakness, the Response is the second person's reply to the Con, the Switch involves a greater awareness of the psychological level implications of the game, and the Payoff is the satisfaction gained from the game outcome.

Game payoffs occur in five types (Karpman, 1972). Each of the five types functions to satisfy certain psychological needs. One of these needs is to prove or reinforce one's existential position arrived at early in childhood: I'm OK — You're OK; I'm OK — You're not OK; I'm not OK — You're not OK; or I'm not OK — You're OK (life positions are discussed in Chapter 3). Another need met by games and payoffs is that of furthering one's life script. Games may be entered into for the purpose of seeking recognition strokes, structuring time, or for collecting psychological trading stamps.

Trading Stamps

The concept of trading stamps, introduced by Berne in 1964, is popular in transactional analysis, and is analogous to commercial trading stamps. Berne (1972) discusses the analogy and notes that commercial trading stamps are a bonus obtained through a legitimate transaction such as a purchase. People have favorite colors of stamps and they may refuse to collect any other kind; they may paste them in books daily or let them accumulate to paste in all at one time; they may redeem them in small quantities for small premiums, or may save them over a period of time for larger prizes. Although some people know that commercial trading stamps are not free and that the cost of the stamps is incorporated into the cost of the merchandise, others do not wish to acknowledge this and prefer to think they are getting something for nothing. Those persons who wish to feel they are getting something free or have a great need to accumulate many stamps may resort to acquiring counterfeit stamps. People enjoy discussing their stamps, the quantity they have saved, and the relative value of different colors of stamps.

Paralleling commercial trading stamps, psychological trading stamps are the by-products of legitimate personal transactions, and people tend to have a favorite color of stamp. There are red stamps (mads), brown stamps (hurts), blue stamps (guilt), and gray stamps (fright) (Berne, 1964b). People may be serious brown stamp collectors and may, therefore, reject other color stamps or turn other colors into counterfeit brown stamps. An example would be a person who received a legitimate gold stamp (compliment), "I really enjoyed being with you today," into a brown stamp, "I always knew that you usually don't enjoy my company," because that's the only kind of stamp they find useful or care to collect. Individuals may go over their stamp collection daily, or they may review it only once in awhile, or they may think about it only when they have nothing else to do. They like to discuss their collection and show it off to others. As with commercial trading stamps, some people know that psychological trading stamps are not free, that they have their price: others do not wish to bother with stamps at all and want to engage in "straight" transactions only; still others need the stamps so badly that they seek counterfeit ones. Berne (1972) notes that the value of collecting stamps rests in the kinds of premiums one can obtain. He states,

> For one or two "books" the person that can get a small prize, such as a free ("justified") drunk or sexual fantasy; for ten "books" he can get a toy (unsuccessful) suicide or an adultery, and for one hundred "books" he can get one of the big ones: a free quit (divorce, leave treatment, quit job), a free go to the mental hospital (colloquially known as a free crazy), a free suicide, or a free homicide. [p. 142]

Referring to trading stamps, Karpman (1972) comments,

> It was previously believed that people bottled up feelings until one day they would explode, but now it is thought that people save up different colored trading stamps and then cash them in for a desired prize at an intended redemption store. These are called Feelings Rackets, and games are played to collect the psychological trading stamps which are the currency of these rackets. For instance, a man needing only two more books of mad stamps comes home from work, starts a fight with his wife, collects the two books of mad stamps, and cashes them in at the bar for a justifiable drunk. [p. 142]

People may give up their Feelings Rackets and rather than red, blue, brown, or gray stamps, begin to collect gold stamps which are also redeemable for small or large prizes. These prizes, however, represent personal joy or accomplishment. Berne (1972) refers to real and counterfeit gold stamps when he says that people think they are collecting gold stamps for the feelings of righteousness, triumph, and joy. Since, according to Berne, only joy is a genuine feeling and not a game payoff as are righteousness, triumph, and other "good" feelings associated with satisfaction through superiority, genuine gold stamps are associated only with joy and acceptance; other "good" feelings may be merely counterfeit gold stamps.

As mentioned earlier, games may be played for the payoff of recognition strokes. Strokes may be positive, negative, or crooked (Karpman, 1972). Positive strokes feel good, negative strokes are hurtful, and crooked strokes are negative strokes disguised as positive strokes. Strokes and recognition hunger are dealt with more fully in Chapter 3.

Time structuring and the possibility of receiving strokes are related in that the availability of strokes is proportionate to the level of personal investment required in social intercourse. Of the six ways that people structure their time (withdrawal, rituals, pastimes, activities, games, and intimacy), withdrawal affords the least opportunity for stroking, intimacy the greatest. Since intimacy is difficult for most people and impossible for others, games are the next best stroking source.

In summary, games are a series of ulterior transactions which progress toward a predictable payoff. Initiated through what appears to be a social level complementary transaction between Adults, the crucial message in games is the unspoken psychological message sent to the Child or Parent ego state. The psychological communication becomes more evident when the "switch" in the game occurs. The switch sets up the payoff. Games are played for the purpose of furthering one's script, for collecting trading stamps, structuring time, gaining recognition strokes, or reaffirming one's existential position. The kinds of games an individual engages in are clues to his life script.

Script Analysis

How one unconsciously plays out his life drama is referred to as his script. Scripts are analogous to theatrical plays in that they have a cast of characters, of which the individual is the star; they contain lines so that the characters will know what to say to each other and how to say it; there are settings, scenery, and acts; and there is a plot. In Berne's (1972) discussion of this analogy, he notes that as with theatrical plays, scripts have a limited number of themes or plots. Even though there are a number of ways to play out a theme, the general course of events follows a predictable plot and the outcome is predetermined. In script analysis, the therapist learns about the plot through the patient's behavior, ego states, games, etc.; and knowing the plot and, therefore, the required cast of characters, he also knows what the outcome will be without therapeutic intervention.

Scripts like dramatic plays call for certain kinds of persons to fill the roles of the characters. Also, in order to carry out one's script, the characters' lines that fit the drama must be strictly adhered to, for if the lines are changed, then both the plot and the outcome changes. In his book on script analysis, *What Do You Say After You Say Hello?* (1972), Berne amusingly illustrates this point:

> All scripts, whether in the theater or in real life, are essentially answers to the basic question of human encounter: "What do you say after you say Hello? The Oedipal drama and the Oedipal life, for example both hinge entirely on this question. Whenever Oedipus meets an older man, he first says Hello. The next thing he has to say, driven by his script, is: "Wanna fight?" If the older man says "No," Oedipus has nothing further to say to him, and can only stand dumbly wondering whether to talk about the weather, the condition of the current war, or who is going to win in the Olympic games. The easiest way out is to mumble "Pleased to meetcha," "*Si vales bene est, ego valeo,*" or "Everything in moderation," and go on his way. But if the older one says "Yes," Oedipus answers: "Groovy!" because now he has found his man and he knows what to say next. [p. 38]

As with drama, the script must be learned, rehearsed, and played out. During childhood, the individual learns the lines of his script; late childhood through adolescence is spent rehearsing and practicing the script; and the rest of his life is spent living his drama.

All scripts have four basic characters: "good guys," "bad guys," "winners," and "losers." Good guys and bad guys are necessary for the games; winners and losers carry the theme. James and Jongeward (1971) define winners and losers as follows, ". . . a winner is one who responds authentically by being credible, trustworthy, responsive, and genuine, both as an individual and as a member of society. A loser is one who fails to respond authentically" (p. 1). Further, they state that losers live in the past and future but not in the now, they fail to respond to inner conflicts, and for the most part are alienated from themselves. Losers frequently structure their lives to insure failure whether consciously or unconsciously. In the language of transactional analysis, winners are called "princes" or "princesses," and losers are "frogs." As Berne (1972, p. 37) states, "The object of a script analysis is to turn frogs into princes and princesses."

In addition to the script there is a counterscript, parts of which most people tend to follow if they are able. The counterscript is comprised of messages representing certain life goals parents have for their children which are socially acceptable and personally beneficial such as "go to college," "seek happiness," and the like; contrasted to these are the "don'ts" of parental injunctions: "Don't show your feelings," "Don't think of sex as pleasurable," or "Don't get close to people." Script messages are stronger than counterscript messages and eventually become the controlling force (Karpman, 1972).

Scripts represent the life drama one unconsciously plays out to its conclusion. Scripts are determined by parental messages and injunctions, as well as attitudes and feelings about oneself and others. Scripts have a limited number of themes or plots, but all have a predictable ending. Berne (1972) sees one object of script analysis to be fitting a patient's plan for life into the psychological history of the human race which is reflected in mythology and fairy tales. He notes that Freud, Jung, and Adler also saw the repetition of mythological plots, the triumph of heroes, as well as the reenactment of fairy tales, heroic deeds, and tragic endings occurring in every day life (p. 57).

Summary

Transactional analysis is a system of psychotherapy based on the analysis of ego states, personal transactions, games, and life scripts. Ego states are phenomenological realities representing accurate recordings of transactions, both verbal and nonverbal, that occur during childhood, with parents and other authority figures, and in reality testing. Every person has three ego states: the Parent, the Adult, and the Child.

There are four distinct but overlapping phases in transactional analysis. Structural analysis is concerned with recognizing and understanding ego states. Transactional analysis serves to clarify what is happening between two persons when they engage in conversation by utilizing the P-A-C diagram. Transactions may be complementary, crossed, or angular or duplex ulterior transactions. Game analysis deals with ongoing, predictable chains of transactions which are initiated on a social level but have a simultaneous psychological level of communication. Games involve a Con, a Gimmick, and a crucial point called the Switch which leads to a psychological Payoff. Script analysis refers to the process of learning the nature of one's predetermined life drama: the plot, the characters, and the manner in which one is moving toward its predictable ending.

3

The Transactional Analysis
Theory of Personality

The transactional theory of personality is also a theory of life
(Berne, 1972). That is, it is a theory about life scripts. Crucial to the
theory are the transactions that take place during the first five years
of life, for the product of those transactions is the unconscious decision the child makes regarding his existential life position. Furthermore, the transactions plus parental scripting provide the
child with the basis of his life drama: the theme, the characters, and
the general movement of the plot. Certain factors, however, are
influential in shaping the child's personality before he is born.

Prenatal Influences

Berne (1972) believes that certain factors exert an influence on
the development of the personality prior to birth. He includes such
determiners as genes and primitive imprinting as well as influences
from ancestors, the conceptive scene, birth order, birth itself, and
forenames and surnames.

Ancestral influence comes not only from direct and indirect messages present in the Parent ego states of the mother and father

which will be passed on to the child, but also from the fact that the parents-to-be may hold hopes that their child may in some way be similar to one of their revered progenitors. This wish will be reflected in the behavior they exhibit toward their child. On the other hand, they may have unconscious fears that the child will inherit certain traits that they find distasteful. This, too, will be communicated nonverbally to the child.

The conceptive scene, with all the accompanying feelings and attitudes on the part of the father and mother, is an important factor in the development of the personality. It may be that one or both of the partners engaged in purposefully deceptive behaviors, or that the impregnation may have not been wanted by either or both parties, or any set of circumstances which may unconsciously affect positively or negatively the behavior exhibited by the parents toward the child. Birth position is important in that it may or may not fit into the parents' scripts to have a child at that particular time. The child may not be the right sex, or he may be poorly timed; he may need to become the football player the father has always wanted; or he may need to fulfill a specific role in the lives of his parents. Birth itself has an effect on the life of the child, not only because of what is referred to as the "birth trauma," but also because the mother may recount her own suffering or unusual circumstances during the birth over and over, generating feelings of guilt within the child. Forenames can be influential in four ways: when they are purposefully chosen (such as unusual names, names of famous people, names of parents); accidental (as girls with boy's name and vice versa); inadvertant (nicknames acquired as a small child); or inevitable (surnames that are "funny," or difficult to pronounce, or that translate into obscenities). Berne sees these factors as having an influence on the personality of the child before birth; they are present from the moment of conception on throughout the child's life.

The First Five Years

"Each normal human infant is born into the world with the capacity to develop his potentialities to the best advantage of himself and of society, to enjoy himself and be able to work productively and creatively, and to be free of psychological disabilities" (Berne, 1966, p. 259). In TA language, this means that each child comes into the world feeling OK.[1] Soon after birth, this feeling is jeopardized

[1] OK is TA terminology for psychological health. Further explanation of OK-ness and the OK-not-OK life positions appear in the section entitled "Life Decisions" in this chapter.

because of the shock the infant receives when he must begin to function on his own in a cold, strange environment. Within a few minutes, however, as the infant is wrapped in a blanket and spoken to softly by the nurse or doctor, he receives his first "strokes," or physical comforting. Harris (1967) considers the time at which the infant receives his first strokes his "Psychological Birth."

The infant has no vocabulary with which he can explain his experiences; he has only feelings. These feelings are continually being recorded in his brain along with other environmental stimuli as he is able to perceive them. Breast feeding, for example, may provide conflicting sets of feelings: OK feelings when hunger is being satisfied, when the warmth and softness of the mother's skin is felt, when pleasurable feelings accompany sucking; not-OK feelings may arise from the same situation such as when the infant's nose is pressed shut by the mother's breast and he experiences a suffocating feeling, or when his appetite is satisfied and mother continues to push the nipple in his mouth. What is important here is that the infant is being stroked, and he is attaching OK or not-OK feelings to the stroking. Also he is making emotional judgments about himself and the person doing the stroking. Berne (1966) believes that when the infant first comprehends that the breast is separate from himself, that is the awakening of the neopsyche or the Adult.

Breast feeding, toilet training, and other experiences which are a part of the life of the small child are sources of good and bad feelings, some about himself, some about other people in his environment. Also, these experiences are accompanied by verbal and non-verbal messages from the child's parents which are recorded in the child's Parent. The feelings the child experiences are similarly being recorded in his Child ego state. These early transactions pave the way for games between child and parent, and provide part of the outline for the life script that is to follow. Berne (1972) suggests that early script programming comes from short scenes at the time of breast feeding with such titles as "Public Performance," "Hurry Up," "It's Not Time Yet," "While Mother Smokes," to name but a few; and toilet training scenes such as "Come and See How Cute," "You Can Just Sit There Till You Do," "Naughty Naughty," and "That's a Good Boy," as well as "That's a G-o-o-d Boy," (p. 83).

Along with these early transactions, another thing is happening to the child. From the initial stroking that occurred when the newborn infant was first touched by another human, there results a feeling of comfort and pleasantness which is associated with physical intimacy. During the first year of life, the infant receives strokes, or physical intimacy, when he is being fed, changed, bathed, or cuddled. Receiving strokes becomes equated with experiencing a feeling of well-being. To relieve the boredom of being alone or the unpleasantness of being hungry, wet, or otherwise uncomfortable, the child develops a stimulus hunger, particularly for physical intimacy. During infancy and early childhood, stimulus hunger is satisfied by stroking in the literal sense, by physical stroking. Later, when physical contact is less appropriate, stimulus hunger is replaced with recognition hunger, and stroking is received symbolically through verbal expressions, facial expressions, and various nonverbal communications. It is important to note that strokes generate warm, good feelings; however, there are negative strokes, or discounts, which have powerful adverse effects. Negative strokes can take the form of frowns or sarcasm, or they can be neglect, abuse, or similar behaviors. One discount has a tremendous effect on an individual, and may be neutralized by no less than four strokes. The ratio of strokes to discounts received by a child will determine whether he becomes a mentally healthy, free, and spontaneous individual or a sociopath.[2]

Life Decisions

The child, then, responding to stroking, discounts, feelings evoked through early transactions, as well as verbal parental messages, begins to draw some conclusions about himself and others around him. He develops a conviction about himself which is either "I'm OK" or "I'm Not OK"; and he also formalizes his convictions about others which may be "You (They) are OK," or "You (They) are not-OK," (Berne, 1966). Life positions are based on the decisions that are made about oneself and others. The four possible positions (Harris, 1967), therefore, are:

1. I'm not-OK — You're OK
2. I'm not-OK — You're not-OK
3. I'm OK — You're not-OK
4. I'm OK — You're OK

Berne (1972) believes the initial position to be "I'm OK — You're OK." Harris (1967) on the other hand, believes that every child assumes the "I'm not-OK — You're OK" position tentatively during the first year of life, and by age three either confirms that position or moves to position two or three. Harris further states that the first three positions are decided upon on the basis of stroking or non-stroking, and are nonverbal conclusions (p. 43).

[2] J. Kovacevich. Lecture delivered at TA Workshop, Toledo, Ohio, November, 1973.

Berne (1966) states that every game, script, and destiny is dependent upon the position chosen, and that each of the positions has certain connotations for action.

I'm not-OK — You're OK

Berne (1972) considers this a depressive and self-abasement position; the position of the "If Onlys" and "I Should Haves" (p. 87). Persons in this position have a great need for recognition or stroking, and try very hard to gain the approval of others. Harris (1967) discusses two ways in which people attempt to live out this position: through a life script that confirms the not-OKness, or with a counterscript with borrowed lines from the parent, "You can be OK, if" (p. 45). Unfortunately, the need to confirm the not-OKness is strong, and therefore the individual spends a great deal of his time failing, collecting trading stamps, and devaluing his accomplishments.

I'm not OK — You're not OK

This position is assumed on the basis of nonstroking. In the total absence of OK feelings, an individual in this position may give up hope and feel that life is not worth living. The outcome may be commitment to a mental hospital, extreme withdrawal, or suicide (Berne, 1966; Harris, 1967; James and Jongeward, 1971).

I'm OK — You're not OK

Berne (1972) sees this position as the "get rid of" position. Persons living out this position play the game of "Blemish" in an attempt to demonstrate how inferior everyone else is. Harris (1967) believes that this position is a product of child abuse or extreme stroke deprivation. The source of OKness, therefore, must come from the child himself as he finds comfort in being alone and in the absence of cruel treatment. Persons in this position vary in their scripts. They may strive to eliminate evil by becoming missionaries or engage in political or religious activities, or they may resort to hostile acts against society such as delinquency, crime, or homicide (Berne, 1966).

I'm OK — You're OK

Harris (1967) believes that this position can be decided upon only verbally and consciously after one decides to give up the games which perpetuate the *I'm not OK — You're OK* position held by most individuals. Berne (1972) on the other hand, believes that this position is either assumed in childhood, or is acquired later in life through hard work and therapy. Berne concludes that this is a basically healthy position which allows individuals to cope with difficulties, be loving and warm, and to engage in authentic relationships. This is the position that allows individuals to move from games to intimacy.

The child, then, having formed definite ideas about who he is (as he has been told by others), how he should behave, and whether he is a winner or loser, has made an existential decision about himself. He also has made a similar kind of decision about others. Through these two decisions he has chosen his life position. At this time, he begins to wonder, "What happens to someone like me?" (Berne, 1972). Seeking to find an answer to this question, he may find that he identifies with a character in a fairy tale or myth, or a fictional hero. Having found a story about "someone like him," he also has found his script. He now has a rough sketch of how to structure his time, what kind of characters he will need to play the roles in his drama, and he unconsciously knows the plot and final outcome of his script.

The actual groundwork in scripting lies in parental injunctions. These are nonverbal messages which have been recorded in the Child ego state, and which have been sent by the parent of the opposite sex. The parental injunctions are true scripting messages which are described by Karpman (1966) and illustrated through the use of the Script Matrix (Figure 6).

FIGURE 6
The Script Matrix

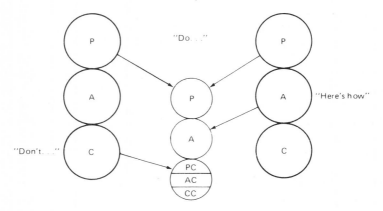

From S. Karpman, *Current Psychiatric Therapies: 1972*, 1972, Grune & Stratton, Inc. Reprinted by permission.

According to Karpman, the scripting process involves both parents telling their child's Parent verbally, "Do be honest (a man), (a woman), (independent), etc." The same sex parent demonstrates how to behave to carry out the messages. The parent of the opposite sex, however, is sending nonverbal scripting messages or injunctions which say, "Don't be honest (a man), (a woman), (independent), etc." The verbal messages which are sent by both parents are collectively called the counterscript. The counterscript calls for behavior which is in opposition to the script, and although parts of the counterscript may be fulfilled, the script is the most powerful and always overcomes the counterscript.

Fairy tales, myths, legends, favorite true or fictitious stories, as well as parental injunctions provide the framework and theme for the life script that has its origins in early childhood. The drama will develop, be refined, and played to its predetermined conclusion.

Later Childhood

At age six, the child has only an outline of his script. He is not sure what it means, but he begins the task of finding out. Even though he is not conscious of it, he has already decided upon his existential position as well as what kind of feelings he will work for (his racket), what kind of stamps he will collect, and he is beginning to form habitual behavior patterns that will ensure the fulfillment of those decisions.

During this time he is also in the process of testing childhood illusions against reality. He is testing out the games he has learned at home in the school setting, hanging on to some favorite ones, eliminating those which are ineffective, and refining his skills at gamesmanship. He is hearing messages from his Parent and his Child; and, to the extent to which he can mobilize his Adult, is sorting, retaining, or rejecting those messages in the face of reality. He is busy learning the lines of his script, and making tentative movements towards finding out what kinds of people will fill the roles adequately.

Adolescence

This is the period for script rehearsal. It is a difficult time because a number of things are happening: parents are no longer structuring time and the adolescent must do it for himself; sexual feelings are new and he is uncertain how they fit into the script or how to respond to them other than with familiar and habitual feelings, his racket; he is replacing the fantasy figures of his script with more workable, real ones; and he is searching for his real identity. He struggles with his script and his counterscript; he struggles between following parental precepts, and rebelling against them. By the end of adolescence he has made the decision to either follow the precepts or to go toward his script payoff (Berne, 1972).

The rest of the individual's life is spent living his script and affirming the life position chosen during childhood; or, the individual may free himself from his script and move toward more personal freedom and greater psychological health, referred to in TA as "getting better."

Time Structuring

An important factor in the development of the personality is the need for time structure, an outgrowth of the need for physical intimacy, or stroking, during infancy. As mentioned earlier, the need for stroking persists throughout life. The infant finds pleasure in physical intimacy; however, as time progresses, physical stroking may be withdrawn or become inappropriate. The hunger for physical intimacy, therefore, is replaced symbolically and the outgrowth is recognition hunger.

The child learns that some sequences of events provide greater satisfaction for the need for recognition than others; he also learns that waiting for sequences to be completed is frequently more satisfying than immediate gratification. The need for recognition, therefore, develops into a strong need to structure time in a fulfilling way through various social transactions.

People structure time in six ways (Harris, 1967): withdrawal, rituals, activities, pastimes, games, and intimacy. Each of the six has certain stroking possibilities. Withdrawal within this context refers to removing oneself psychologically from a social situation into fantasy for the purpose of self-stroking by recalling or imagining satisfying and pleasurable encounters. Rituals are socially and culturally approved standards of social behavior which require no personal commitment. Berne (1964a) notes that people usually base the number of strokes given and received in rituals on the frequency of opportunities to engage in the ritual and on the relationship between those involved. They come to expect no more or no less than the expected number of strokes, and any deviation from the standard would tend to arouse suspicion. Activities are means for dealing with material reality in ways which fulfill one's particular personal or professional role in life without intimate involvement. Activities may provide a source for stroking, or they may be used by some primarily to avoid intimacy. Pastimes are ways of structuring time congenially but noncommittally, such as cocktail parties, bridge parties, luncheons, clubs, or when people are waiting for something to begin as a concert, a meeting, or the like. Sources of stroking while engaging in pastimes come from pride in ownership, personal accomplishments, and mutual interests. Pastimes may be Adult-Adult, Parent-Parent, or Child-Child, but whatever the level, they are harmless and personally rewarding. On the other hand, games usually are destructive and may or may not be rewarding; but they do provide strokes. Games involve all the components of the personality, and require a "con," a "gimmick," a "switch," and a "payoff." Games may serve a defensive function, or they may be employed to meet the needs of the Parent or Child ego states (Berne, 1966). They are necessary for the advancement of one's script toward its ultimate goal. Intimacy, the greatest source of stroking, is achieved through nondefensive, authentic relationships and is independent of the previously mentioned ways to structure time. It occurs when the Adult is in charge, the Parent is recognized but not inhibiting, and the Natural Child is allowed to emerge (Harris, 1967).

The Acquisition of Maladaptive Behavior

The psychologically healthy person is one who is able to segregate his ego states, maintain permeable boundaries for ease of movement from one ego state to another, and can appropriately cathect an ego state according to the presenting situation or transaction. The psychologically disturbed person is unable to do this because of structural or functional reasons (Berne, 1961).

Exclusion

Structural pathology may be due to either *exclusion* or *contamination*. Exclusion is the habitual, stereotyped cathexis of one ego state in response to threatening situations to the exclusion of the other two. The constant-Parent seeks to exclude the Child through control and denial. Rarely, and only under the most favorable circumstances, is the Child allowed to emerge. The same exclusion and denial by the constant-Parent of the Adult ego state holds true, for it would be threatening to deal with reality and face the possibility of finding Parent messages untrue. The constant-Adult is cold, deliberate, organized, and rigidly logical. There is no spontaneity or fun-seeking because of the excluded Child; there is an inability to assert a position or take sides because of the excluded Parent. The constant-Child is narcissistic and impulsive. Rational and realistic messages from the Adult are ignored, and controlling or moralistic messages from the Parent are denied. The excluded ego states are said to be *decommissioned.*

Contamination

Contamination occurs when one ego state intrudes upon and influences another ego state, notably the Adult. The Parent-contaminated Adult results in prejudiced behavior. Regardless of how realistically the Adult attempts to perceive something, Parental influences bias the perception. Sweeping generalizations are made on the basis of Parent tapes. The Child-contaminated Adult suffers paranoia or delusions. The archaic feelings of the Child distort the data-processing of the Adult. The Adult may be doubly contaminated by both the Parent and the Child (Berne, 1961).

Functional Pathology

Functional pathology is observed when an individual habitually moves rapidly from one ego state to another, or when the ego states are so weakly bounded that they all seem to flow together. This condition is observed typically when an individual seems to be "overreacting" or is described as "flighty." Another type of functional disorder occurs when there is difficulty in moving from one ego state to another, or it occurs in a slow manner (Berne, 1961). This condition may be observed as stubborn persistence (difficulty moving from Parent), whining behavior (difficulty moving from Child), or seeming detachment (difficulty moving from Adult), or similar kinds of overt behavior.

Maladaptive behavior is a result of traumatic or fixating experiences occurring at some point in time during one's lifetime. As each day's experiences are recorded and programmed into the ego states, some may be so powerful that they have an effect on the perceptions of the ensuing days' events. This tends to be cumulative, and results in increasingly greater distortion unless a compensating event occurs which rectifies the situation. Berne (1961) compares a day's experiences (an ego unit) with coins, and likens a traumatic experience with a warped coin. The effect on the personality is shown in Figure 7.

Summary

One's personality is developed and expressed within a social context. Transactions are units of social contact, and through trans-

FIGURE 7
Effects of Traumatic Ego Units on Ensuing Ego Units

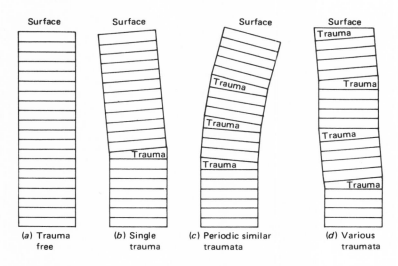

(a) Trauma free   (b) Single trauma   (c) Periodic similar traumata   (d) Various traumata

actions the ego states are activated. Transactions occur in several forms and serve to satisfy the need for time structure, an outgrowth of physical intimacy needs and recognition hunger. One way of structuring time is to engage in a series of ulterior transactions, or games, which satisfy certain personal psychological needs at the expense of others.

During the first five years of life, the child learns to replace the physical intimacy of infancy (stroking) with units of recognition (symbolic stroking). He also is recording his experiences in his Parent and Child, and is beginning to some degree, to activate his Adult. Through his transactions he is forming ideas about himself and others which culminates in a decision, or life position, concerning the OKness or not-OKness of "I" and "They." Energies are thereafter devoted to confirming the chosen position.

Once the life position has been decided upon, the child then wonders what life holds in store for "someone like him." He finds the answer when he identifies with a character in a fairy tale, myth, or legend. Then, on the basis of the story, the Child's experiences, the Parenting messages, and the position chosen, the child develops a life script, or the way in which he will live out his life drama.

Ego states are the focal point of transactional analysis since their recorded verbal and nonverbal messages, the degree to which they can be distinguished, the permeability of their boundaries, and the relative strength each has developed, influence not only the formation of the personality, but also are crucial to personal functioning.

4

Transactional Analysis
in Practice

The transactional analysis approach is most effective when used within a group setting. The language is simple and easily taught, and it provides the group members with a common vehicle for communication. The social transactions within the group provide the therapist and the patient the material with which to work. Group members are first instructed in the language of transactional analysis and then in understanding structural analysis. This initial step may take place in the group, or members may be instructed individually prior to taking membership in a group. Initially, patients need to learn only six words in order to understand structural and transactional analysis: Parent, Adult, Child, pastime, game, and script. Additional colloquial phrases or terms may be added as the patients progress or as they seem appropriate in understanding more complex transactions. The next crucial step involves learning to identify ego states, not only within oneself, but as they are evidenced in others. The patients, possessing now a common, working language and rudimentary knowledge of ego states, are ready to learn transactional analysis, a basic tool for further progress in self-knowledge, analysis of games and scripts. As Berne (1961, p. 165) states, "The objective of transactional analysis in group therapy is to carry each patient through the progressive states of structural analysis, transactional analysis proper, game analysis, and script analysis, until he attains social control."

Preparation for Group Sessions

In general, groups are heterogeneous rather than homogeneous in transactional analysis, and no particular selection criteria is used for patients other than in those instances where it would be obviously inappropriate to place a particular patient in a particular group. The decision regarding special placement may be made at the conclusion of preliminary interviews with patients, the purpose of which is to determine readiness for therapy. Also, during the preliminary interviews, the therapist and patient come to a contractual agreement. The contract consists of a statement by the patient regarding why he is there and what he wants to accomplish for himself, and a statement by the therapist of what he is able to offer and what his expectations are for group members.

Case histories and previous therapy evaluations are not considered useful for they represent another person's impression of the patient, and the patient may have chosen to present himself differently in the previous situation. His current presenting behavior is the focal point of therapy rather than past behavior. Of importance, however, is knowledge of the physical condition of the patient, medication he may be taking, and other conditions which may have a direct bearing on his ability to benefit from therapy. Psychological tests are also considered biased and unfair to the patient, and are used only in rare instances, such as when a rapid diagnosis is essential.

Research is discouraged in groups whose primary aim is therapy. Berne (1966) claims that research which is done openly has a detrimental effect on the process: the group members are more concerned about what is going to be done with the material collected than they are about getting better. Furthermore, research done without the knowledge of the patients, or hidden research, is dishonest and less than desirable. Therefore, research should clearly be undertaken only in groups designated for that purpose and should be differentiated from therapy groups. Tape recordings for the purposes of supervision have the same effects on good therapy as do recordings made for research purposes, but the end result of better performance by the therapist justifies the use of a recorder.

The Group at Work

Berne (1963) considers five members in a group an absolute minimum and believes that more than eight (Berne, 1972) prevents the therapist from attending to every individual. Berne further states that sessions should be from one and one-half to two hours in length, and continue over a period of no less than seven weeks. The therapist's role should be strong and distinctly different from those of the members.

Transactions in the group, either between individual members or between a member and the therapist, provide the vehicle for therapy. As stated earlier, group members have a language available to handle psychological terms and concepts, and they have a basic understanding of ego states. They are now ready to begin analyzing transactions. Berne (1963) states,

> An elementary classification of chains of transactions which is particularly useful to beginners in group therapy is the triad discussion-description-expression. Discussion is concerned with the external environment (pastimes and activity). Description is concerned with personal feelings — talking about them rather than expressing them; these are Adult descriptions of Child and Parent attitudes and are often part of a game of Psychiatry. Description is often marked by the use of "this" in place of "that" as a demonstrative ("This is what I did yesterday" rather than "That is (or was) what I did yesterday.") Expression refers to the direct, undiluted expression of feelings toward another member of the group. [p. 177]

As transactions occur, patients are taught to become aware of the kind of transaction taking place and the ego states involved. The therapist makes frequent use of the P-A-C diagram to represent graphically the transaction and to provide further information about the dynamics of the ego states.

As the group progresses, attention is given to the games exhibited by individual members. Of particular interest are those games played by any particular patient which may appear in different forms but have similar substance, and games which the patient plays consistently in a variety of situations. It is important that the patient become aware of the fact that even though games may initially seem to provide external social gains, they are actually a means to deal with inner conflicts, sexual gratification, reassurances, and defenses (Berne, 1961). Once this understanding has been attained, advanced structural and transactional analysis becomes appropriate, and the relationship of the games to the patient's life script is investigated. Overall, transactional analysis is primarily aimed at life scripts; however, script analysis is slow and psychoanalytic. Therefore, script analysis is the last phase of therapy, for this theory holds that individuals should "get better first and analyze it later" (Berne, 1972, p. 303). This point of view regarding the need for analysis represents one of the points of departure between transactional analysis and psychoanalysis. The transactional analyst believes that the patient must first be "cured" before analysis can be meaningful. To be cured means that he has fulfilled his therapy contract and has established reasonable social control. He is able to activate ego states appropriately, has given up or modified his games so that they are no longer destructive, and has developed a strong, active Adult. These conditions are essential if the slow process of analysis is to be beneficial and effective. Furthermore, many individuals are not psychologically disturbed enough to need extensive script analysis and are able to function adequately once they give up their games.

Utilizing the Four Components

Although the four components of transactional analysis (structural, transactional, game, and script analyses) blend together into one therapeutic process, each of them is useful for specific treatment. In a recent article, Karpman (1972) discusses developments in transactional analysis and the utilization of the four kinds of analyses at various points in the treatment process.

Structural analysis, as mentioned earlier, is used to acquaint the patient with ego states and prepare him for further therapy. Later, it can assist the patient in learning to listen to the internal dialogues between ego states, or his voices in the head, and to allow his Adult to start a new dialogue. It is also utilized in decision making by examining and evaluating the needs of the individual ego states; in looking at and diagramming the various facets of the personality; in determining whether any of the ego states limit or distort one's perceptions of his world; and as a way of categorizing external events. In some extreme cases where the Parent is especially destructive, structural analysis is used in reparenting, which is the process of erasing old Parent "tapes" and replacing them with more useful messages.

Transactional analysis as a technique is used to diagram ways in which an individual typically interacts with others such as in role playing or when he is stuck in a particular ego state. It also can be used to depict blocks to communication and listening which are the result of crossed transactions; to give and receive feedback within the group about how one is "coming on"; and to learn new response options. Patient progress can be shown by diagramming the way in which he is using more and more of the nine available ways of communicating effectively with others (Figure 8). Representing graphically the bilaterality of relationships is useful in helping individuals understand not only that another person is involved in his problem, but also that he may be giving another person permission to intensify his problem.

Karpman (1972) states that certain types of transactions that appear in the group are emphasized because of their importance. One of these is the "Gallows Transaction" in which the patient smiles and winks when he is talking of his failures ("Well, I think I took another step toward skid row last night, ha, ha.") and gets the other patients happily smiling back, thus acquiring group permission to continue on his failure script. Another is the "Discount Transaction" whereby Adult functioning is discounted by a Parent in one of four ways (p. 139):

a. There is no problem.
b. The problem is insignificant.
c. There is no solution to the problem.
d. Nothing can be done by me to solve the problem.

FIGURE 8
Nine Possible Channels of Open Communication

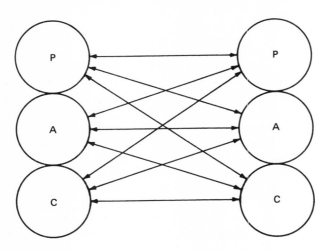

In therapy, game analysis helps focus on the reality of what is going on, as well as expand one's awareness of the dual nature (psychological and social) of behavior. The patient, through game analysis, becomes aware also of the relationship of individual events to a chain of events or transactions leading to a game payoff. It is also helpful for the patient to learn to identify certain feelings that accompany game stages. Becoming aware of feelings that accompany being "hooked" (accepting the invitation to participate in a game), the switch, and the payoff prepares patients for future game transactions. They can refuse to get hooked; or if they do get enticed into game participation, they have the option of either continuing knowing in advance the possible switches and payoffs and preparing for them, or discontinuing the game.

As mentioned earlier, in script analysis, if the therapist knows the plot and the cast of characters of a patient's script, he can predict the outcome or ending of the life drama. In therapy, most of these scripts call for a tragic ending, and only through therapeutic intervention can the tragedy be averted. Helping the patient become aware of the plot and the predetermined conclusion is one of the most valuable uses of script analysis. Once this has been accomplished, the patient then can become aware of behavior, internal and external influences, and games which serve to fulfill the script requirements.

Another valuable use for script analysis is to avoid "Hot-Potato" scripting, or passing one's script on to one's children because of Witch Messages that are not identified or understood by the patient (Karpman, 1972).

Procedures and Techniques

In addition to instructing patients in the knowledge and use of the four phases of transactional analysis as well as diagnosing ego states, the therapist also is looking for script signs and clues to parental programming and past experiences which have determined the nature of the script (Berne, 1972). The most effective and important tool of the therapist is observation (Berne, 1966, 1972), and it is used in every phase of the therapy. Observations of physiological phenomena are interpreted psychologically, and the effective and alert therapist will not only be attuned to overt behaviors but will also be able to detect incipient stages of behaviors. The broad diagnostic categories are body attitude, tone of voice, vocabulary, and effect on others (Karpman, 1972). Observation is made of breathing, blushing, tremors, perspiration, emotional reactions, as well as posture, movements, gestures, and voice quality, to mention only a few of the diagnostic signs.

Facial Expressions

Facial expressions are especially telling as most persons are unaware of their changes in expression; even the slightest movement of eyes, mouth, jaw, brow, and so on, may provide information to the therapist. It is especially important that the therapist note any inconsistency between verbal statement and facial expression. Gestures are classified as symbolic, emphatic, exhibitionistic, or functional (Berne, 1966). Of greatest interest are the functional gestures for they are archaic in nature and reflect personal idiosyncracies. In observing gestures, facial expressions, and attending to the verbal message, the therapist may note that all seem consistent with one another, indicating a well-organized personality; it may be, however, that two may be inconsistent with the other, or all three appear incongruent. Berne (1966, p. 68) notes that ". . . typically, the Adult ego state may say one thing in words, the Child ego state may say another thing through facial expressions, and the Parental ego state may convey its sentiments through gestures."

The observation of script signs is first done intuitively by the therapist's Child, and later recognized by his Adult. Script signs such as tics, characteristic gestures or mannerisms, are responses to a Parental directive and occur unconsciously in specific situations. Posture, carriage, and clothing also may provide clues to an individual's script (Berne, 1972).

Vocal Signals

Listening is another tool of the therapist. Not only does the therapist listen to the word content and gross vocal clues, he listens as well to the more subtle aspects of the verbal message including pitch, rhythm, tone, and vocabulary. Listening to content is done by the therapist's Adult while how it is said is heard by the "Professor" or the Adult in the Child (Berne, 1972).

Four basic vocal signals are sounds, accents, voices, and vocabulary (Berne, 1972). Sounds include different types of breathing sounds such as coughing, sighing, giggling, and laughter. Laughter is categorized into the scripty laughs of the three ego states and the healthy laughter of each of them (Berne, 1972). Accents are clues to Parental precepts. Each of the ego states has its own voice which is distinctly different from the other two. Usually at least two of the voices can be detected while listening to an individual over a period of fifteen minutes (Berne, 1972). Three vocabularies correspond to the ego states also: borrowed (Parental) which is indicated by highly stylized, mannered, or affected speech; the conceptual, intellectual, externally focused vocabulary of the Adult; and the Child's vocabulary of expletives, "tough talk," baby talk, and expressions of rebelliousness (Berne, 1966).

The Parent, the Adult, and the Child all contribute to the sentence structure and content of what an individual says; therefore, transactional analysts find transactional parsing valuable (Berne, 1972). Transactional parsing consists of attending to sentence construction and the choice of words which indicate ego state influence and origin. The therapist will listen for parts of speech (adjectives, adverbs, nouns, etc.), O.K. words (words approved by the Parent of a parental figure), script words (words related to script theme and roles, frequently slangy or obscene), metaphors, security phrases (words or gestures which are used ritualistically before speaking), subjectives (if, if only, would, could, should, and noncommitment words), and for patterns in sentence structure (Berne, 1972).

Observing and listening skills are basic to good therapy and essential in identifying ego states, as well as in script analysis. They are used in conjunction with eight categories of intervention techniques: interrogation, specification, confrontation, explanation, illustration, confirmation, interpretation, and crystallization (Berne, 1966).

Intervention Techniques

Interrogation is directed toward the patient's Adult and is used to document pertinent points, for example, "Did you believe that behavior was useful?" Questioning is not used if it seems likely that the patient's Parent or Child will respond; however, it may occasionally be useful to use questions to determine which of his ego states will respond, as a checkpoint for progress.

Specification is used to categorize information in order to fix it in the minds of both therapist and patient for future reference. Specification may include statements such as "So that is another social situation in which you feel uncomfortable," or "That sounds more like your Child than your Adult." Specifications must clearly reflect a statement or a behavior of the patient. It is important that what is specified does not threaten the patient's Child, although this technique may be applied to determine the degree of threat the Child can handle.

Confrontation is used to point out inconsistencies and the purpose of the technique is to draw out and strengthen the uncontaminated Adult. Using previously specified information, the therapist uses confrontation to redistribute cathexis of the ego states. A therapeutically successful confrontation is evidenced by obvious changes in behavior which indicate that the Adult is in command; a poorly worded or ill-timed confrontation serves to strengthen the inappropriate ego state which is already in operation.

Explanation is helpful in strengthening the patient's Adult by providing a rational and realistic account of the inner dialogue and dynamics of his Parent and Child. It may be particularly effective when a patient is perceived as being on the verge of giving up his games.

An *illustration* is a story, comparison, or similar type of presentation that follows a successful confrontation and it serves the purposes of reinforcing the confrontation. Illustrations may be immediate and therefore provide the opportunity for further cathexis, or delayed (remote) in which case they are used to further therapeutic growth. There are internal and external illustrations, with internal illustrations referring to group members and external illustrations related to activities outside the group. Illustrations should be lively, and should be in simple language that appeals to the patient's Child as well as to his Adult. Berne (1966) states that illustrations should be understandable to a wise five-year old; and that the vocabulary should primarily consist of two and three syllable words, with prudent but deliberate use of colloquial terms.

Confirmation of behavior by the patient's Adult, following confrontation and illustration, further reinforces ego boundaries. It may be, however, that the Child is not quite able to give up the inconsistencies stated in the confrontation. Following a successful confrontation but with the Child still exercising some control, the therapist may sum up the events of the confrontation and illustration and then confirm the fact that the Child is still attempting to override the Adult.

The preceding techniques have the objective of cathexis and decontamination of the Adult (Berne, 1966). With the Adult strengthened and in the executive position, the task is now to deconfuse the Child. The therapist may use the technique of interpretation or he may use crystallization or a combination of the two to undertake the task of deconfusing the Child. Using *interpretation,* the therapist speaks to the uncontaminated Adult of the patient, sorting, decoding, removing distortions, and clarifying childhood experiences. A *crystallization* is a statement of the patient's position from the Adult of the therapist to the Adult of the patient. This technique is more or less a statement of task completion and recognition that the patient now has a choice of giving up or continuing his games, and also the choice of exercising Adult control over situations. The enthusiastic acceptance of the therapist's crystallizing statements by the patient's Adult, Parent, and Child is an aim of transactional analysis, and is indicative that the patient is ready to choose whether or not he wants to "get better." In other words, it is the beginning of social control.

Other therapeutic interventions mentioned by Berne (1966) include support (simple stroking), reassurance (from the therapist's Parent), persuasion, and exhortation (appealing to the patient's Child). It should be noted that techniques are constantly evolving out of the current practice of transactional analysis. Although the newer tools may be a modification of the basic techniques and interventions, they are given colloquial names which are descriptive of what is happening. One such intervention is called "Rubberband" (Kupfer and Haimowitz, 1971), which is dependent upon the therapist's intuition. A Rubberband is a snap-back to childhood feelings being expressed in the here and now by the patient, and can be recognized by an overreaction to some stimulus or by an inappropriate response on the part of the patient. The therapist may respond to the patient's archaic feelings by sharing with the patient a fantasy of what the therapist thinks might have happened during childhood, or he may translate the fantasy into an Adult response, or he may stay in the here and now in a Gestalt therapy fashion. TURN-OVER (Miller and Maloney, 1972) is a procedure in which the therapist asks the patient to turn a statement into the direct opposite of what he has just said. The therapist remains neutral and gives no indication of what the opposite may be. The purpose of the technique is to assist patients in understanding more of their internal dialogue.

A useful tool in game and script analysis is the Karpman Triangle (Karpman, 1968). As mentioned earlier, each person plays out his life drama, or script, and the drama calls for a cast of characters. Karpman states that most dramatic roles can be recognized as either a persecutor, a victim, or a rescuer. These roles can be legitimate in that they are assumed because of real situations; however, when they are assumed for the purpose of manipulation they become illegitimate roles. The three roles make up the Karpman Triangle (Figure 9). Using capital letters to differentiate manipulative roles from legitimate roles, James and Jongeward (1971) give examples of the three as on both levels:

persecutor: Someone who sets necessary limits on behavior or is charged with enforcing a rule.

FIGURE 9
The Karpman Triangle

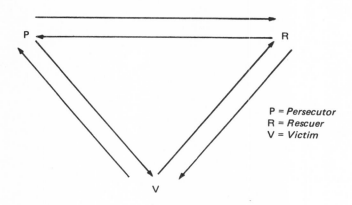

P = *Persecutor*
R = *Rescuer*
V = *Victim*

Persecutor: Someone who sets unnecessarily strict limits on behavior or is charged with enforcing the rules but does so with sadistic brutality.
victim: Someone who qualifies for a job but is denied it because of race, sex, or religion.
Victim: Someone who does not qualify for a job but falsely claims he is denied it because of race, sex, or religion.
rescuer: Someone who helps a person who is functioning inadequately to rehabilitate himself and stand on his own two feet.
Rescuer: Someone, who in the guise of being helpful, keeps others dependent upon him. [p. 88]

In games, switches in roles occur and are an important part of the payoff. An example of how the Karpman Triangle works would be a three-handed game such as "Let's You and Him Fight," or simply the person caught in the middle of a situation between two other persons. One person (Victim) approaches another person (Rescuer) and relates how unfair and less than understanding the third party (Persecutor) has been. The Victim asks the Rescuer to assist him by talking to the Persecutor and trying to set things straight. This the Rescuer does, and the outcome is that the Rescuer becomes the Victim of the previous Victim, who is now the Persecutor, assuming things did not work out to his advantage. Further discussion of the use of the Karpman Triangle will be presented in Chapter 5.

Decontamination

Ideally, the Parent, Adult, and Child ego states are separate, have distinct but permeable boundaries, and the messages recorded in the Parent and Child are undistorted and useful. The Adult, also ideally, has been used frequently enough to build up its strength so that it can be called into action when the Parent and Child are at odds with each other, or when either of them emerge with inappropriate behavior. The efficiency and effectiveness of the Adult, however, is reduced when it is contaminated by either the Parent or the Child or both. Contamination of the Adult by the Child occurs when archaic ideas and feelings which belong in the Child have invaded the Adult boundary and have been rationalized by the Adult as being Adult feelings and ideas (Berne, 1961). This type of contamination produces delusions; paranoia is a severe form, and believing people are talking behind one's back is symptomatic of milder contamination. Parent contamination of the Adult in its severe form results in hallucinations, or a powerful feeling of being above the law; a case in point would be one who advocates or actually participates in ridding the world of a race, cult, or similar group he believes he has been called on to eliminate. Lesser contamination manifests itself as prejudice. The Parent-contaminated Adult has accepted Parent messages as true without checking out the reality of the situation objectively.

Decontamination occurs when the patient's Adult understands the situation, realizes that certain ideas or feelings are relics of childhood or messages from parenting tapes, and is able to make decisions for himself through his objective Adult which assumes personal responsibility for the decisions. After decontamination has taken place, it is then necessary to strengthen and clarify the boundaries of the ego states. This may be done by talking to the specific ego states of the patient one at a time (Berne, 1961). Another important consideration in the decontamination process is what Berne (1961) refers to as actionism, or the strengthening of the Adult with use. Patients are assisted in learning to bring the Adult into control, and to maintain the Adult as executive for increasingly longer periods of time.

Listening to Voices in the Head

The observable behavior of an individual reflects expression of ego states in some final common pathway (Berne, 1972). The final common pathway may be selected by dissociation, in which case each ego state expresses itself independently and unconsciously, as noted earlier in the example of an individual's incongruent or conflicting words, expressions, posture, etc. Secondly, it may be selected by exclusion wherein one ego state constantly takes over expression for the other two. Or thirdly, it may be selected through integration with all three ego states expressing themselves at once congruently. The selection of the final common pathway is the result of an internal dialogue between ego states, or voices in the head. The voices in the head are there because of actual words that have been heard; and the inner dialogue, especially the Parental directives, determine what one will express and how it will be expressed. The therapist, through listening and observing, becomes aware of the nature of the voices and assists the patient in learning to listen to them and relate them to the therapist. In order to do this, he must give the patient "permission" to hear the voices and to disobey Parental injunctions. Berne (1972) refers to permission as the decisive intervention in script analysis.

Permission is not needed when the Parent has already sanctioned a behavior. However, when the Parent is prohibiting an expression of the Child, or taking energy from the Child, and the Adult is too weakly cathected to intervene, the therapist provides outside assistance and strengthening messages for the Adult. In order to do this, the therapist first of all must make contact with the patient's Adult, form an alliance with his Adult, mutually agree on a plan to give the patient's Child permission to disobey his Parent, and provide the support necessary to see the patient through the consequences (Berne, 1972).

In summary, the process of transactional analysis includes four distinct phases: structural analysis, transactional analysis proper, game analysis, and script analysis. The role of the therapist is that of teacher, observer, listener, and interventionist. The most effective tools of the therapist are listening and observing which provide the information about the patient that is necessary for analysis and intervention, and for determining the nature of the patient's script. The therapist uses the intervention techniques of interrogation, specification, confrontation, explanation, illustration, confirmation, interpretation, and crystallization, as well as permission and decontamination. Transactional analysis holds that instructing the patient in structural, transactional, and game analysis is of primary importance, for individual understanding and control of one's behavior precedes analysis and personality change.

Training and Preparation for Practice

The transactional analysis therapist should be trained in psychoanalytic theory and practice, transactional analysis, group theory, and group dynamics; the therapist should also have an understanding of existential therapy, gestalt therapy, Jungian psychology, and psychodrama (Berne, 1966). In addition, it is recommended that the practitioner supplement his didactic training with personal individual and group therapy in order to develop the level of self-awareness necessary to understand what is happening to group members during the course of therapy. Adequate supervision during training is deemed essential. Standards for training have been established by the International Transactional Analysis Association Training Committee. Of the six levels of membership available in ITAA, only the fifth and sixth levels (Clinical Membership and Teaching Membership) carry the privilege of practicing Transactional Analysis. Initial admission to membership in ITAA on an Associate Member level requires evidence of professional qualification as a psychiatrist, psychologist, psychiatric nurse or social worker, correctional officer, social scientist, or clergyman; or graduate student status in one of the fields of social psychiatry. Selected undergraduates may be accepted.

Research

The clinical and empirical data supporting the principles and structure of transactional analysis have been mentioned elsewhere. Outcome research indicates that transactional analysis not only compares favorably with other effective therapies, but in some instances is highly efficient in producing positive results. Transactional analysis is based upon the belief that the contents and condition of the ego states are directly observable through overt behavior and expressed attitudes. Therefore, the criteria for success in therapy are behavior changes, integrated and healthy ego states which can be given executive power at appropriate times, and a strong uncontaminated Adult.

In an early study (Berne, 1957) involving 23 psychotics and pre- and post-psychotics, and 42 patients not falling in those categories, treatment extending over a two-year period and utilizing structural analysis resulted in 78 percent improvement in the group of patients in the psychotic categories, with 10 percent failure and 12 percent showing no change. Results for all other patients who made up the second group in the study indicate 67 percent improvement, 33 percent no change, and no failures. Further research of this nature is difficult to find in the literature; however, Berne's publications (1961, 1963, 1964a, 1966, 1968, 1972) as well as the *Transactional Analysis Journal* contain numerous case studies and illustrations which indicate the method is significantly effective based on the criteria of observable change in behavior, giving up games, strengthened and used Adult, as well as verbalized changes in attitude and outlook on life. It is important to note that fulfillment of the therapy contract is one measure of "success."

Lack of research data may be due to the fact that the theory is relatively new and has only recently become more widely used. There has been, however, limited research investigating the OK — not OK life positions. Thamm (1972) investigated factors related to the four basic life positions: I'm OK — You're OK; I'm OK — You're not OK; I'm not OK — You're OK; and I'm not OK — You're not OK. Seeking to find those variables related to acceptance of self and acceptance of others, Thamm administered a 129 item questionnaire to 434 college undergraduates. The questionnaire was divided into sections dealing with demographic data, subject perceptions of parents, deprivation areas in Maslow's need hierarchy, defense behaviors, self-expression, emotional states, and attitudes. Dividing the data into six levels of self-acceptance and acceptance of others, the results indicated that there was a significant and direct relationship between accepting oneself and accepting others. The study yielded general descriptions of personalities fitting into the categories, but not predictors.

In another investigation of life positions, Allen (1973) administered two measures of existential position, the *Interpersonal Evaluation Inventory* and the *Existential Position Inventory,* and the *Rotter Incomplete Sentence Blank* measure of adjustment and emotion. The Ss were 111 undergraduate psychology students. The results generally support the relationship between position and adjustment. Significant correlations were found between I'm OK — You're OK and good adjustment, while the I'm OK — You're not OK and I'm not OK — You're OK positions were related to maladjustment. No significant relationship was found between I'm not OK — You're not OK and adjustment. In addition, I'm OK — You're OK subjects reported significantly more positive emotion and less anxiety and depression. I'm OK — You're not OK subjects showed less anxiety and depression but more boredom, findings which are compatible with Thamm's results which indicated that persons in this position tend to be intelligent, not deprived of personal satisfaction, but tend to withdraw from social interaction.

As more work is done in the area of transactional analysis and as the theory is applied to a variety of situations such as educational settings as well as clinical practice, research findings should begin to fill the void that now exists.

5

Application in the Schools

The simplicity, concreteness, and language of transactional analysis all contribute to the usefulness and ease of application of its principles in the school setting. It is essentially a teaching-learning model which is easily adapted to either the classroom or counseling setting. TA has wide appeal because the concepts can be quickly learned and understood by persons of all ages, and it is suitable for use with persons of limited intellectual ability. Transactional analysis can be helpful in working with individuals and with groups of students, teachers, and parents. Its principle functions in the school would be to develop an understanding of self and others, and to promote more effective communication between individuals. Nelson (1972) states that the transactional orientation toward analyzing messages sent and received, anticipating the effects of messages, and developing more effective ways to communicate, are appropriate goals for counseling (p. 145).

This chapter will deal with the topics of structural, transactional, and game analysis as they apply to school counseling and guidance; the utility of TA language; extending the concepts of transactional analysis to parents and teachers; and transactional analysis in the classroom.

It should be understood that the principles of transactional analysis should be used as tools for understanding people and what people do, and for promoting improved communication. It cannot be overemphasized that correct identification of ego states is vitally important; therefore, it is recommended that counselors who wish to implement this approach read the major works of Berne, and if possible, attend a workshop or seminar in transactional analysis.

Structural Analysis

Counselors frequently hear students and teachers express a desire to understand another person's behavior that is puzzling for one reason or another. And just as frequently, counselors hear students and teachers make judgments about others or categorize them on the basis of certain behaviors. It is sometimes difficult for them to separate a behavior they dislike from the person himself. Students may refer to a person as "bossy," or "hard to talk to because they always have to be right," or as "a big baby." Teachers may refer to students as "immature," "childish," "stubborn," or "a troublemaker." All too often, the repetition of a behavior that triggers a strong reaction in another person, or even one isolated bit of behavior, leads to a decision about the nature and the worth of the person displaying the behavior. One method of approaching this problem is to employ structural analysis. By becoming aware of the three ego states and the fact that any of them can gain executive power, either by choice or in response to a set of circumstances, it is possible for individuals to realize that people are capable of several kinds of behavior. For example, a student who dislikes another student because he is so "bossy," may find this behavior more tolerable if he can say to that student, "I like you, but I sure have trouble liking your Parent." Furthermore, this kind of communication clearly indicates that it is a particular behavior that is disliked, not the person himself. An additional benefit from messages focusing on ego states is that the person receiving the message becomes aware of which ego state is in charge, and this frequently is instrumental in mobilizing the Adult.

Becoming aware of one's own ego states and learning to diagnose them properly is equally as important as knowing about others' ego states. Because movement from one ego state to another is largely unconscious, it is helpful to have someone call attention to the fact that the Parent or Child has emerged and may be interfering with what he is doing or saying. To illustrate this point, consider the elementary school student who comes to the counselor and, on the verge of tears, states that his teacher doesn't like him and won't help him with a difficult assignment. It is apparent that his Child is feeling hurt and helpless. In talking with the student, the counselor can help him become aware of what his Child is feeling, and that what the student really wants perhaps is to have the teacher acknowledge the fact that the lesson is hard for him. His Child would also benefit from some strokes to relieve the feelings of inadequacy. Rather than continuing to harbor resentful feelings toward the teacher, the student is able to discover the source of the feelings within himself. The student now has the choice of continuing to let his Child's reaction to the situation make him feel miserable, or he may wish to approach the problem more realistically by encouraging his Adult to ask the teacher for assistance in understanding the assigned lesson.

Students of any age may be "stuck" in an ego state, or, as discussed earlier, be a constant-Parent or constant-Child; or some may be a constant-Adult as seen in the aloof, analytical, and non-socializing student. Since each of the ego states has its accompanying set of words, gestures, facial expressions, and attitudes, it is possible to practice or rehearse the expression of ego states. The counselor may wish to ask the student to think about how his own parents act and speak, what gestures he remembers them using frequently, and what words they use. Or he may assist him in recalling his childhood experiences and the feelings that accompanied them. Listing behaviors and vocabularies, gestures and expressions that belong to the various ego states is an initial step in beginning to use, and therefore strengthen, each of the ego states. As the individual role plays the part of a parent, adult, and child, he begins to become familiar with how it feels to express his Parent, Adult, and Child. In doing so, he is expanding his knowledge of himself, his possible means of communicating with others, and he begins to attain greater flexibility in his behavior.

Structural analysis can be used in individual counseling sessions to promote self understanding and personal expression. It also can be used in group counseling and in classroom guidance activities. It would be particularly effective to instruct students in structural analysis in the classroom prior to individual or group meetings for that would facilitate the counselor's work and the student's program.

Transactional Analysis

Students and teachers alike are aware of the fact that there are some people they can talk with easily and comfortably, and there are others that seem to cut off communication almost before it gets started. They are also aware of encountering persons who say one thing but actually mean something else. What they may not be aware of is that they are experiencing daily different kinds of transactions, and that each of the transaction types elicits predictable responses and outcomes. Understanding the nature of complementary, crossed, and ulterior transactions does not necessarily mean that communication problems will cease, but it has the potential to alleviate misunderstandings and blocks to communication.

The counselor can utilize the analysis of transactions any time that there is a gathering of two or more people. The gathering could be a classroom group, a faculty meeting, parent-teacher conference, or counseling group to mention but a few of the possibilities. Of course, the necessary prerequisites are the prior knowledge of structural analysis and the desire to improve the communication process on the part of the participants. The role of the counselor in the previously mentioned situations excluding counseling would be that of a consultant. The counselor would not participate in the group meeting, but would observe, listen, diagnose ego states, and diagram the transactions that appear to have a significant effect on the proceedings. It is not enough, however, for the counselor to indicate the originating ego states and the type of transaction which has occurred. The participants of the group should also be given the opportunity to experiment with alternative responses by repeating the transaction incorporating the behaviors and vocabularies of other ego states and noting the outcome as well as their personal reactions to each combination of ego state transactions.

In addition to working with transactional analysis *per se* in a consulting role, the counselor can assist groups of students and teachers in learning to become aware of the typical mode of response each of them uses in certain kinds of situations. Presenting a number of hypothetical situations, the counselor might ask that each person write down the first response that comes to mind. Patterns of responses for individuals, or responses that consistently originate in the Parent or Child can be diagrammed and alternative ways of responding can be practiced and discussed.

The counselor can gain insight into the dynamics of teacher-student relationships within the classroom by analyzing the transactions that take place. Is the teacher consistently a critical-Parent or nurturing-Parent, or does his Child appear frequently and inappropriately? What kinds of behaviors on the part of the students seem to "hook" the teacher's Parent or Child? What effect does the teacher's behavior have on the modes of responses available to the students? The transactions that take place may reflect cooperative efforts between students and the teacher through a series of complementary transactions and sustained communication, or they may reflect disharmony and conflicts as Parent and Child engage in a power struggle of crossed transactions.

The combination of structural analysis and transactional analysis can provide the counselor with valuable tools for helping students understand what people do and why they do it. Students also can begin to understand their own behavior, and through this understanding, develop the ability to choose ways of behaving and responding in a variety of situations. The same kinds of insights into their own behavior on the part of teachers, as well as a better understanding of the effect of their behavior on students, permit the teacher to become more effective in the classroom and minimize the number of personal conflicts that interfere with the teaching-learning relationship.

Game Analysis

Since the appearance of Berne's *Games People Play*, the word and the concept of *game* have become commonplace in describing behavior. When one becomes aware of a personal involvement that he finds puzzling or confusing, or when he finds he has been "taken in" by someone who uses him to further their own needs or interests, he has become the victim of a game. To avoid the recurrence of such uncomfortable and unpleasant situations, it is necessary that he become knowledgeable about the dynamics of games and the course of events that produce games.

Nearly everyone plays games on occasion. Students, teachers, administrators, parents, and even small children indulge in game playing. Some of the games are harmless, but some of them are destructive, especially when played by a serious gamesman. Games follow a predictable course toward a predictable outcome or payoff. For this reason, the general play of the game does not change according to the age of the player or the setting, it is merely adapted to fit the immediate needs of the situation. The counselor reading *Games People Play* can readily identify adaptations of most of the games described in the book being played out in the classrooms of the school daily.

Student Games

In his book *Games Students Play*, Ernst (1972) has translated adult games into student games and has described the series of moves which lead to the payoff. Ernst categorizes student games as 1) trouble-maker games, 2) put-down games, and 3) tempter games. Trouble-maker games are those games that interfere with the teaching process; put-down games specialize in one-upmanship and giving negative strokes; and tempter games serve to manipulate teachers into positions which assure that they will end up losers.

Trouble-maker games come in two varieties: disruptor type and delinquent type. The disruptor variety includes the games of "Uproar," "Chip on the Shoulder," "Stupid," "Clown," "Schlemiel," and "Make Me." Nearly every teacher has experienced an "Uproar" player: the student who taps his pencil, coughs, moves about, and makes a series of small disturbances that continue until the teacher can no longer tolerate the situation and yells at him. The student protests that the teacher is unfair for lashing out at him for "just dropping my book," for the student asserts that it was only the last small incident, not the whole series of incidences, that provoked the teacher into responding unreasonably. Ernst (1972) describes the "Chip on the Shoulder" player as a student who wants to avoid something. He speculates that the student wishes to avoid being faced with his own lack of intellectual ability. In order to cover up his vulnerability, this player becomes the class show-off who is capable of creating a disturbance each time the teacher calls on him to respond to the lesson being presented. The antithesis of this game is to discover what the student is trying to avoid and then to assist him to deal with his vulnerability realistically.

"Stupid" players make deliberate dumb moves when there is an audience present to witness and enjoy his "dumbness." "Stupid" players can be identified by the smile that comes over their face as they do something dumb. The last thing a teacher should do is to say, "That was a stupid thing to do." The "Stupid" player likes the strokes he gets from his performance, and having his moves confirmed by the teacher as stupid provides even more strokes.

The "Clown" player, as compared to the "Chip on the Shoulder" player is harmless and isn't avoiding anything (Ernst, 1972). He is well-liked, playful, and enjoys getting strokes by being amusing. He seems to be able to determine when it is appropriate to entertain and when it is not.

Both the "Schlemiel" player and the "Make Me" player are interested in the responses their games evoke. Both games serve to challenge the respondent into being either a Persecutor or a Rescuer. "Schlemiel" players "accidentally" destroy or mess up someone else's property. If the teacher lectures him about respecting the property of others, the response is considered that of a Persecutor, and the player protests that he is being treated unfairly for something that happened accidentally. If the response is that of a Rescuer, who is sympathetic and tells the owner that "he really didn't mean to do it," the player takes that as permission to repeat similar acts. The "Make Me" player is not too subtle. Take, for example, the student who consistently fails to do his homework. If the teacher keeps him after school or in some way makes him do the work, he is being persecuted. If the teacher compromises or backs down, then the student has won the power struggle and is ready to challenge the teacher soon on new ground. Ernst (1972) suggests that teachers make clear to students the choices they have available regarding their school responsibilities, the consequences of the choices, and then leave it up to the student to decide on his course of action and to be fully responsible for his choice.

Delinquent disruptor games, according to Ernst, are related to identity struggles and are played by those students who need to "leave their mark." "Let's Find" something to do is played by those persons who need to structure their time. What they find to do may be harmless or destructive. "Cops and Robbers" frequently appears where strict rules have been laid down. The players openly flaunt the rules and challenge the teacher or principal to be a Persecutor (enforces rules and penalties) or a Rescuer (makes an exception after eliciting a promise from the student to follow rules in the future). The "Want Out" student tries desperately to get suspended from school, get kicked out of class, or be removed from some situation. As the threats become stronger, he plays harder. Finally, when it is apparent that he is indeed going to be suspended or removed from class, he pleads for "one more chance." Will the teacher or principal become a Persecutor or a Rescuer? Either way, the teacher or principal is being set up for another round of the game. The way to avoid that situation is to refuse to play the game although human nature and the vulnerability of the Parent ego state make it difficult to resist the temptation.

Put-down games may be of the discount variety or the complainer variety. Discount games include "Sweetheart" and "Blemish." "Sweetheart" involves giving out insults which are disguised as strokes in order not to violate the politeness society demands, or it may involve disguised disagreements. "Blemish" is played by persons who do not feel OK about themselves. They find real or imagined faults with others in an effort to prove that everyone else is not OK either, or at least no more OK than they.

The complainer variety includes the student who sets up a situation which is sure to cause him difficulty (misplace or lose a library book, lose his homework, forget an assignment, etc.) and then waits to be called upon to be held responsible for the problem, and feels personally persecuted for his bad luck. He's playing "Why Does it Always Happen to Me?" The "Indigence" player appears to keep trying to understand an assignment or to complete his work on a project, seems to be exerting effort to understand and maintain concentration, but succeeds mostly in evoking feelings of frustration in the teacher who is rapidly exhausting the number of ways in which help can be offered. The student who engages in "Late Paper" always seems to have reasonable excuses for his procrastination. "Wooden Leg" involves relying on a disability, illness, unusual circumstances, or other apparently reasonable excuse for not being able to meet the teacher's expectations for acceptable work. "Why Don't You — Yes But," a popular game in any setting, has been discussed elsewhere.

Teacher needs for admiration or dependency makes them susceptible to Tempter games such as "Disciple" and "Li'l Ole Me," both of which are variations of "Gee, You're Wonderful Professor" (Ernst, 1972). The success of "Disciple" depends upon the teacher's willingness to be idolized; and the game of "Li'l Ole Me" is almost impossible to play without the willingness on the part of the teacher to be manipulated by charm and/or helplessness into giving higher grades.

The Trap-Baiter variety of Tempter games (Ernst, 1972) includes games that can be more serious. "Miss Muffet" is played by the person who sits by calmly waiting for someone to commit an innocent indiscretion. The incident is blown up and distorted by the player, and the person who unknowingly erred ends up a victim of "Now I've Got You." "Miss Muffet" is typically a female game as are "Stocking" and "Rapo," both of which are sexual games. Played by females who need to maintain the position that men are not OK, "Stocking" and "Rapo" can have serious consequences for the unsuspecting male teacher or counselor.

The "Do Me Something" player challenges the teacher to teach him. He wins by refusing to learn. He challenges the counselor by implying, "You know about behavior. Change mine." If the counselor does in fact take on the responsibility for changing the player's behavior, he, too, will lose.

Counselors frequently are placed in the game of "Let's You and Him Fight." How often students complain to the counselor about a teacher, and the counselor decides to intervene on the part of the student. The student plays one against the other until misunderstanding and distorted messages bring the game to its culmination.

The student has succeeded in getting the focus off himself and he's enjoying watching the counselor and the teacher try to pick up the pieces of a situation he created.

Teacher Games

As mentioned before, nearly everyone plays games and this includes teachers. Ernst (1972) specifies three categories of teacher games: "Close-to-student," "Helpful," and "I Know Best."

"Close-to-student" games originate in the teacher's Child who wants strokes from students. The games include "Buddy," needing to feel popular with students and meeting that need by doing "in" things or being lax in requirements; "Self-Expression," a foil used to pry into the details of students' lives; and "Critique," the game of encouraging students to come to the teacher for advice or to tell him their problems simply because he likes to hear those kinds of things. He does nothing, however, but listen and make judgments.

"Helpful" games serve the teacher's or counselor's nurturing Parent. A favorite one is "Student Folder" wherein the students' records are searched in an effort to find the certain causes of student behavior or learning problems. "I'm Only Trying to Help You" has been discussed elsewhere; it is all too frequently a counselor's game. "Sunny Side Up" players are unrealistically happy and sweet regardless of what happens. They delight in keeping the peace and since they do it so well, students make sure there are arguments to be negotiated. The teacher who plays "Education" tries all the principles of education in an attempt to achieve classroom control. If there are problems, they can be solved by improving the learning climate through bulletin boards, seating arrangements, and the like. The real problem may be a matter of poor pupil-teacher relationships, but that area lies untouched. The teacher who is insecure attempts to find out if he's doing a good job by playing "Look How Hard I've Tried." Student failure equals personal failure as a teacher for players of this game. To impress other teachers, the LHHIT player exhausts himself by providing students with extra help, extra work, and puts in long hours preparing lessons.

The critical Parent in the teacher plays many games, all in the "I Know Best" category. One of the more common is "Furthermore." Teachers who collect mad stamps save them for a game of "Furthermore." What happens is that a teacher's patience is exhausted and overcome by a small incident. In the process of reprimanding the student for that particular infraction, the teacher "furthermores" a whole series of past situations that he is still begrudgingly hanging onto. The more he elaborates on past behaviors, the angrier he gets and the more he "furthermores." Another game that unfortunately is seen often is "Professional." The "Professional" player is a teacher who avoids finding out how effectively he can teach. His degree and teaching certificate indicate his qualifications to teach, and if the students don't learn, it's their fault. Teachers using the discovery method of teaching should exercise caution that they are not actually playing "Tell Me This" and wasting the students' time with phrases like "You're Getting Closer," or "Warmer." Other teacher games in this category include "Courtroom," "Now I've Got You," "Corner," and "See What You Made Me Do," all of which are highly descriptive of the action taking place in the game.

The Challenge to the Counselor

All these games may sound familiar for they do occur in schools everywhere. The challenge to the counselor is not to identify games or describe what game a person is playing: that is a game in itself called "Psychology." The challenge is to assist teachers and pupils in stopping games by helping them learn how to refuse to play or by learning to incorporate the antithesis of the game.

Counselors can assist teachers by helping them understand not only the moves of the games but also how they allow themselves to get involved in the play of the game. An important consideration is that game players capitalize on another person's weaknesses. Students are adept at playing games and their first task is to find the nature of the teacher's weakness. Students are particularly concerned about the nature of the teacher's Parent for this determines the ease with which they can manipulate him. If the teacher is unaware that his vulnerable spots are obvious, he will be the victim of game after game.

The counselor can help the teacher discover what games are being played and can assist him in learning about his weaknesses by having him utilize the "Game Plan" (James, 1973, p. 195). The teacher should note:

1. What keeps happening over and over again?
2. How does it start?
3. What happens next?
4. And then what happens?
5. How does it end?
6. How do you feel after it ends?

If the teacher isn't aware of the fact that games may be going on but does know that his classroom is a source of anger and frustration for both him and his students, the counselor may wish to observe the classroom in action. If the teacher and the students are repeatedly engaging in certain behaviors that consistently have the same outcome, then games are in process.

The next step for the counselor then is to help the teacher become aware of how he is responding to the games, and to learn new responses that will end the games. Ernst (1972, pp. 19–28) has listed several types of teacher responses to the student game of "Uproar." The responses may well be generalized to other games and are summarized as follows:

1. The Tyrant Teacher. This teacher responds to students by overpowering them with words or even force. His Parent comes on strong and he reinforces the student's belief that all authorities are unreasonable. This teacher gives out a lot of anger stamps.

2. The Martyr Teacher endures games and suffers quietly. His behavior implicitly gives permission, or even invites repetition of games. This teacher probably collects depression stamps, pities himself, and has a long suffering nurturing Parent.

3. The Whiner Teacher "buys" cooperation with favors, bribes, etc. The effect is temporary and he feels hurt when students do not appreciate all he has done for them. His Child collects hurt stamps.

4. The Scrapper Teacher. Even though the student's game is aimed at this teacher's Parent, his Child intervenes and responds with sarcasm, belittling, name-calling, and similar childlike behaviors. The Child (student)-Child (teacher) conflict can go on indefinitely.

5. The Impatient Teacher can't risk losing control and removes the offender from the classroom at the first move. This behavior merely serves to solve the teacher's immediate problem, nothing else. This teacher's students spend a lot of time in the hall, in the principal's office, in the counselor's office, and in the detention hall.

6. The Timid Teacher is unsure and not OK with himself. He allows the students to rule the classroom, indulge in games at will, and may even allow them to embarrass him in front of other teachers or the principal. He is fair game for all players.

An alternative way teachers can respond to games tends to end them. The teacher can first confirm through the Game Plan that a game is indeed going on. Next, the teacher's Adult explains to the student the game he is playing and how it interferes with his school work and social relationships. He explains his position and responsibilities as a teacher, and he discusses avenues of action from which the student may choose and their probable consequences. When bids to initiate a game begin thereafter, the teacher's Adult can give the student some verbal feedback reflecting the content of what the student is saying as well as the implicit feelings that prompted the bid, and then proceed to refuse to play the game. The teacher must be sure, also, that the student receives the strokes he desires. This should be done between games or before they start, not during a game or after a game has been initiated (Ernst, 1972, p. 28).

In order to help teachers cope successfully with student games, the counselor should become familiar with the dynamics of games. He should read *Games People Play* (Berne, 1964) and *Games Students Play* (Ernst, 1972); and he should become adept in discovering why the individual student plays his game, what he gets out of it, what is the antithesis of the game, and how to turn off the game.

Stopping games before they get started helps the student-teacher relationship and removes some barriers to learning. It does not, however, provide a means for helping students give up their games. This is not an easy task, but movement toward eliminating games can be made by working with students in groups for the purposes of helping them learn more about their games and why they play them. One of the techniques the counselor could use would be to role play games. Observing a role play of a game has the effect of making the moves seem obvious and therefore less powerful to the player. Also, as the social and psychological messages and moves are described and discussed, the game loses some of its attractiveness for the manipulative moves have been exposed. During the course of the role playing, games may be stopped at various key points with alternative behaviors and responses substituted for what usually happens in the game. The students can experiment with the alternate responses and discover the ways in which they change their attitudes as well as the outcome of the game.

Group counseling with students, for the purpose of helping students help each other find new ways to gain the need satisfaction they found in their games, can be valuable. The task is relatively easy if the students play games to obtain strokes or to structure time. It becomes more complex when working with stamp collectors, and the group sessions may need to be supplemented with individual counseling for those students who would benefit from dealing with their need to collect anger, guilt, and other trading stamps. In addition, the counselor may discover during the course of individual counseling that referrals may be in order for some of the counselees.

The Language of TA

Children of all ages, and adults as well, relate quickly to the colloquial terms that are characteristic of transactional analysis. Whole sets of behaviors or concepts, as well as attitudes, that would require lengthy explanations can be communicated through the use of one descriptive word. Children especially find the words useful for the terms tend to capture the essence of an idea which they can readily identify with everyday happenings. It would be a difficult task to try to teach personality theory to elementary school children; but they can use the words Parent, Adult, and Child to convey an understanding of facets of the personality and modes of behavior, and they quickly grasp the concept of games.

The terms stroke and discount (negative strokes) are short and to the point, and incorporate not only a behavior being displayed but feelings and attitudes that accompany the behavior. Counselors are familiar with the student who enters his office and bombards him with what seems to be an endless list of complaints. There may be so many complaints that both the student and the counselor are confused, and a considerable amount of time may be spent sorting things out rather than dealing with the student as a person who is experiencing a distressing situation. If the student were able to say to the counselor, "My Child hurts (or is angry) because I got a lot of discounts I didn't deserve today," the focus of the counseling session is immediately on the counselee rather than on outside events. The session can then progress toward helping the student understand the source of his feelings and ways to deal with them immediately and, hopefully, in the future. Supposing, however, that the student is not sophisticated enough to make such a statement but is familiar with TA terminology. The counselor may then respond to the list of complaints by saying, "It sounds to me like you've received a lot of discounts today. I wonder what that's doing to your Child?" The effect is the same: the focus of the interview is on the student and the feelings he is experiencing at the moment.

The use of TA terms in groups is effective in facilitating communication and expediting the process. Some of the terms counselor find useful are "Warm Fuzzies" (positive strokes freely given with caring), "Plastic Fuzzies" (crooked strokes), and "Cold Pricklies" (negative strokes that hurt). These terms were developed by Steiner[1] in a story called "A Fairytale." Other useful terms are

[1] Copyright 1969, Claude M. Steiner, 35 Westminster, Kensington, California 94708.

marshmallows, rackets, blackmail, hook, and Santa Claus, to name but a few that have not been discussed elsewhere.

"Marshmallows" are Parental supportive statements that actually serve to put off or brush off someone else (James and Jongeward, 1971). Examples include teacher statements to students such as, "I'm glad to hear that you're going to get a part in the school play. Maybe you can tell me about it later," or the student who tells his friend, "You got a neat new bike, but wait til I tell you about what I got!" Some "marshmallows" are simply overly sweet, empty responses that shut off communication.

Rackets have been discussed earlier but will be used again here in relation to "blackmail" and "hook." Certain behaviors tend to evoke Parental or Child responses rather than Adult responses. The equivalent in TA language is to "hook the Child (Parent)." The mutuality of relationships is evident when an individual can say, "You really hooked my Child good that time." Rackets hook the Child and/or Parent easily if the individual being hooked is unaware of what is going on. Becoming aware of how others use their rackets in this manner is to know how to use the term "blackmail." To say to someone, "I won't let you blackmail me with your tears (guilt, yelling, etc.)," not only says that the individual will not allow himself to be hooked, but it also brings the other person's racket into the foreground.

The concept of Santa Claus is related to childhood fantasies that Santa is good and will bring children what they want eventually (Berne, 1972). Although the Santa Claus myth is a part of script analysis, it does present an interesting idea for the counselor to use. Persons who are waiting for something to happen, who can be thought of as persons who could be happy if only something would happen to change their life for the better, can be said to be "waiting for Santa Claus." Many students spend their time waiting for good things to come to them or for school to get easier because of something someone does for them, or for any number of similar things rather than using their energies to get things done for themselves. Exploring the Santa Claus theme may provide the students with insights into their behavior that they otherwise may not get or may reject from parents or teachers who urge them to make their own future.

New terminology is continually developing. Orten (1972) has added new dimensions to the stroke concept by providing stroke-terms for units of recognition that are not face-to-face. Pictures are frozen strokes; letters are canned strokes; and telephone calls become long distance strokes. Memories are called second-hand strokes because they are strokes being used again. Nonexistent strokes which develop from daydreaming or fantasies are termed fairy strokes. Most of the newer colloquialisms arise out of clinical work and may be related to new techniques; some are added to the vocabulary of the approach simply because they vividly describe a recurring social or personal phenomenon that was previously unnamed.

Glossaries of standard transactional analysis terms can be found in Berne's writings (1963, 1966), and numerous other colloquialisms abound in the transactional literature, especially the *Transactional Analysis Journal.*

Transactional Analysis in the Classroom

Teachers and counselors working together can provide a place for the use of transactional analysis in the classroom. As mentioned earlier, the teacher-learner format of the approach allows it to move easily into the classroom setting.

Student games and behaviors arising from the three ego states have been discussed, but there are other applications that are especially appropriate for the classroom setting or for special classes such as the disabled or handicapped. A fundamental belief in transactional analysis is that individuals engage in behaviors that continually reaffirm their existential OK-not OK position. Also, since students have decided at an early age whether they are winners or losers, they tend to structure their activities so that the outcome will fit the ideas they have about themselves. Support for the transactional position related to early decisions may be found by talking to teachers about their students. If one would ask a teacher how different students would approach a task or problem, the teacher would most likely be able to describe the typical behaviors of each of his students in such a situation and predict the outcome. Many would attribute the differences among the students to varying abilities, degrees of motivation, self concept, attitude toward school, or any number of similar factors. Transactional analysis attributes the differences to the individual's life script and existential position.

J. Ernst (1971) reports a study of the effectiveness of transactional analysis in a high school learning disabilities classroom. Hypothesizing that most of the "disabilities" were actually well-developed games based on early OK-not OK positions, the students were asked to identify where they were academically and what they were doing to "goof up." The students were assisted in learning about their script themes, what their "sweatshirt" slogan was, and what games they played and why. *Games People Play* (Berne, 1964) was used as a text, and the P-A-C circles and OK Corral (F. Ernst, 1971) were used in personal problem solving and decision making. At the end of one year 90 percent of the students in the class showed two years' progress in academic attainments, and some students made as much as three years' progress in three months.

The OK Corral (F. Ernst, 1971) is a diagram for assisting individuals in the resolution of personal decision making (Figure 10). Ernst states that people seek encounters with others for the purpose of determing the value they have to themselves and to others. Regardless of the length of the encounter, the outcome is resolved in one of four social operations: Get-nowhere-with; Get-away-from; Get-rid-of; or Get-on-with. The resolution is directly related to the person's life position as indicated in Figure 10. One of the purposes of the OK Corral grid is to help individuals meet problems head on and come to a Get-on-with solution which represents the I'm OK — You're OK position. Behaviors associated with the Get-nowhere-with solution are avoidance, postponement, and relationship blocking. Persons employing the Get-away-from solution find reasons for avoiding invitations to encounter extended by others. The Get-rid-of solution is outright dismissal, while the Get-on-with solution is Adult-oriented, open, and geared to reality.

FIGURE 10
The OK Corral

YOU-ARE-OKAY-WITH-ME

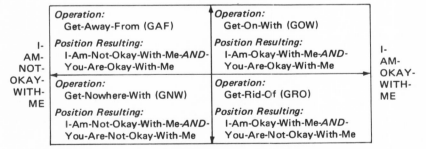

YOU-ARE-NOT-OKAY-WITH-ME

The OK Corral, as well as the other techniques and procedures in transactional analysis, are directed toward allowing persons to become aware of the fact that they have choices to make regarding their behavior and relationships. First of all, however, they must have an understanding of themselves, what they are striving for, and the manner in which they usually move toward their goals. Once they have attained an understanding of themselves, they can be presented with the options they have for action and the outcomes associated with each of them. Since they, then, make the choice, the responsibility for their own behavior lies completely within them. The classroom setting provides countless opportunities for helping students become responsible for their choices of behavior. The value of employing transactional analysis in the classroom lies in providing the students with the tools necessary for making autonomous choices when the opportunities arise.

Counselor Accountability

Persons in TA therapy groups make a contract with the therapist stating their goals in terms of the kinds of behaviors they wish to acquire or give up. When these changes in behavior can be observed and appear to be functional, the person is said to be "cured."

Counselors are being called upon to be accountable. They are being faced with the need to demonstrate that their actions do make a difference. Transactional analysis is built upon observable behaviors; therefore, it is compatible with accountability. If the counselor is doing his work and is doing it effectively, it will be apparent in the changes that take place in student behavior. The attainment of counseling goals can be easily assessed, and the long range effects of counseling can be determined by periodically observing how the student is functioning in the classroom.

Parent and Teacher Groups

Once the counselor has decided to use the principles of transactional analysis with students, it is imperative that he also include parents and teachers, since they are the primary persons with whom children play games. Furthermore, it may be that the games the parents and teachers indulge in encourage more rigorous participation in games on the part of the children. Opening better channels of communication for parents, students, and teachers is a mutual goal of guidance and transactional analysis.

The approach used with parents and teachers is similar to that taken with students. They may, however, need to have more structured activities to help them get in touch with their ego states. Some of the activities could be recalling and role playing early childhood memories, remembering and trying to portray their own parents, taking note over a period of time of the gestures they use consistently, recalling the relationships they had with their parents and what they remember their parents telling them about how they should behave, and keeping a record of the feelings they experience over a period of time, especially the recurring feelings.

Group instruction in structural and transactional analysis coupled with the sharing of memories, feelings, attitudes, and experiences provides a non-threatening atmosphere for learning about oneself. As parents learn more about their own personalities, they become aware of the impact their behavior has on their children. Groups of teachers may gain similar insights into their relationships with their students and fellow teachers.

Parent groups may be more productive if conducted separately from teacher groups, at least initially. Each of the groups tends to look at children differently because of the difference in their relationships with children. After each of the groups has progressed to the point of being able to use their knowledge of transactional analysis in a productive way, the groups could be mixed.

Participation in parent groups or teacher groups would be voluntary. The counselor, however, should encourage teachers especially to become familiar with transactional analysis. In the elementary school where students usually are with one teacher all day, full participation on the part of faculty members is not as crucial as it is in schools in which students meet with several teachers each day. The effectiveness of dealing with student games will be enhanced if the student-teacher transactions are fairly consistent in each of the student's classes.

Advantages and Disadvantages of TA

As with all approaches to understanding human behavior and initiating change, transactional analysis has both positive and negative aspects. The advantages of transactional analysis include these:

1. The concepts and strategies of transactional analysis are easily understood and communicated, and the goals of the approach fit well within the framework of legitimate counseling and guidance goals.

2. Transactional analysis provides individuals with tools for self-understanding, self-initiated change, and for making choices in modes of behaving.

3. The language of TA is familiar, easy to remember, non-threatening, and provides a vehicle for describing sets of behaviors and psychological phenomena for persons not knowledgeable in psychology.

4. Transactional analysis is relatively easy to learn, and for the purposes of use in the school setting, does not require extensive training. The teacher-learner model of the theory adapts easily to classroom use.

5. The usefulness or appropriateness of the approach is not limited to specific age groups nor is it unsuitable for the physically or mentally handicapped.

6. The approach has as its goal swift attainment of social control of one's behavior, and more effective and personally rewarding functioning in society.

7. A distinct advantage of using this approach to counseling is that the effectiveness of counseling and the attainment of counseling goals are reflected in observable changes in behavior.

Some of the disadvantages of the approach are:

1. The basic principles of the theory are expressed in such simple terms that individuals may attempt to implement the approach without adequate preparation.

2. Many persons reject the approach because they find the terminology and jargon unattractive.

3. The effectiveness of using the approach with students is lessened unless parents and teachers and other significant adults in the students' lives are involved and instructed in transactional analysis.

Another advantage of employing transactional analysis is that it provides a vehicle for group work. Counselors who find that they hesitate to work with groups because they feel they have not had adequate preparation or are not comfortable with the lack of structure which is typical of group counseling, may find that the orderly progression of transactional analysis aids them in developing leadership expertise which will allow them to move into other kinds of group activities.

Summary

Transactional analysis as an approach to counseling has a wide range of application in the schools. It is appropriate for use with children in the elementary school as well as high school students, parents, and teachers. Its usefulness is not dependent upon extensive training in the theory on the part of the counselor, nor is it dependent upon extensive knowledge in the field of psychology on the part of the groups who would use it. The effectiveness of the approach can be quickly assessed by observable changes in behavior, and therefore is compatible with the quest for accountability in the counseling profession. It is essentially a teaching-learning model which is easily adapted to the school setting by both teachers and counselor.

APPENDIX

Resources for Counselors

Books and Pamphlets:

*Berne, Eric. *Games People Play.* This best seller describes games, their dynamics, and antitheses. This book provides the background and understandings needed to utilize other publications devoted to games. $1.50 paperback.

Berne, Eric. *The Happy Valley.* (Grove Press, New York. 1968.) This children's book is about a python who earns a living by being nice to people on Tuesday night and Friday morning. $4.95.

*Berne, Eric. *A Layman's Guide to Psychiatry and Psychoanalysis.* A comprehensive guide to transactional analysis, this publication covers all aspects of the theory in an easy to read form. $6.95.

*Berne, Eric. *What Do You Say After You Say Hello?* The theory and practice of transactional analysis is presented in an understandable and often humorous manner. The book contains a comprehensive discussion of scripts, scripting, and how scripts function. $1.95 paperback.

Campos, L. P. & McCormick, P. Introduce Yourself to T.A.: A Primer. (Berkeley, Calif.: Transactional Pubs. No date.) Pamphlet, $1.00.

*Ernst, K. *Games Students Play.* Ernst describes games within the school context, illustrates moves that produce games, and provides suggestions for teachers for dealing with games. $3.95 paperback.

Freed, Alvyn. *T.A. for Kids (and Grown-Ups Too)*. (Berkeley, Calif.: Transactional Pubs. No date.) An easy to read guide to transactional analysis. $4.00.

*Harris, T. A. *I'm OK — You're OK*. A guide to transactional analysis as well as a good discussion of the early decisions regarding life positions and the implications for life functioning. $1.95 paperback.

*James, M. & Jongeward, D. *Born to Win: Transactional Analysis with Gestalt Experiments*. This book is appropriate for use with groups of students in the classroom or in counseling groups. Included are many exercises which help the student become aware of his inner dynamics. An instructor's manual is available. $4.95 paperback, $1.00 manual.

*James, M. & Jongeward, D. *Winning with People*. A workbook devoted to group exercises in transactional analysis. $3.95 paperback.

Steiner, C. *T.A. Made Simple*. (Berkeley, Calif.: Transactional Pubs. No date.) Pamphlet, $1.00.

* See bibliography for publisher and date.
All of the publications listed above are available from:
Transactional Pubs
3115 College Avenue
Berkeley, California 94705

(American Airlines has a pamphlet entitled *P-A-C at Work*, written by L. K. Randall, copyright date 1971. A handbook designed to guide individuals through their daily lives utilizing transactional analysis to understand what is going on in their encounters with people at work, at home, and in their social life. Cost not available.)

Tapes and Instruction Kits

Abbey, D. S. & Owston, R. H. T. *Introduction to T.A.* This kit contains tapes, six booklets describing the P-A-C diagrams, six booklets devoted to games, and a 161 page manual. It may be used with leaderless groups and is suitable for use by persons with little knowledge of transactional analysis. The cost is $50.00. Copyright date, 1973. Available from Human Development Institute, Division of Instructional Dynamics, Inc., 166 East Superior Street, Chicago, Illinois 60611.

Owston, R. H. T. *How to use Transactional Analysis Concepts*. Kit of six audio tapes designed to teach and expand on the fundamentals of TA. For use in classes or groups. Available from Affective House, Box 95, Union, Michigan 49130, at a cost of $64.95.

(Discussion tapes and teaching tapes are available from Transactional Pubs, each about seven hours in length, and costing from $35.00 to $49.00 each. Information will be sent upon request.)

BIBLIOGRAPHY

Allen, J. G. Existential position and adjustment in a college population. *Transact. Anal. J.*, 1973, 3, 202–204.

Berne, E. The nature of intuition. *Psychiatric Quart.*, 1949, 23, 203–226.

———. Concerning the nature of diagnosis. *Int. Rec. Med.*, 1952, 165, 283–292.

———. Concerning the nature of communication. *Psychiatric Quart.*, 1953, 27, 185–198.

———. Intuition IV: primal images and primal judgment. *Psychiatric Quart.*, 1955, 29, 634–658.

———. Ego states in psychotherapy. *Am. J. Psychother.*, 1957, 11, 293–309. (a)

———. Intuition V: the ego image. *Psychiatric Quart.*, 1957, 31, 611–627. (b)

———. Transactional analysis: a new and effective method of group therapy. *Am. J. Psychother.*, 1958, 12, 735–743.

———. *Transactional analysis in psychotherapy.* New York: Grove Press, 1961.

———. Intuition VI: the psychodynamics of intuition. *Psychiatric Quart.*, 1962, 36, 294–300.

———. *The structure and dynamics of organizations and groups.* Philadelphia: J. B. Lippincott Co., 1963.

———. *Games people play.* New York: Grove Press, 1964. (a)

———. Trading stamps. *Transact. Anal. Bull.*, 1964, 3, 160. (b)

———. *Principles of group treatment.* New York: Oxford Univ. Press, 1966.

———. History of the ITAA: 1958–1968. *Transact. Anal. Bull.*, 1968, 7, 19–20. (a)

———. *A layman's guide to psychiatry and psychoanalysis.* New York: Simon & Schuster, 1968. (b)

———. Reply to Dr. Shapiro's critique. *Psychol. Reports*, 1969, 25, 478.

———. *What do you say after you say hello?* New York: Grove Press, 1972.

Cheney, W. D. Eric Berne: biographical sketch. *Transact. Anal. J.*, 1971, 1, 14–22.

Dusay, J. M. Eric Berne's studies of intuition. *Transact. Anal. J.*, 1971, 1, 34–44.

English, Fanita. The substitution factor: rackets and real feelings. *Transact. Anal. J.*, 1971, 1, 225–230.

————. TA's Disney world. *Psychol. Today*, 1973, 6, 45–50.

Ernst, F. H. Jr. The OK corral: the grid for get-on-with. *Transact. Anal. J.*, 1971, 1, 231–240.

————. Psychological rackets in the OK corral. *Transact. Anal. J.*, 1973, 3, 95–99.

Ernst, Jennie Lou. Using transactional analysis in a high school learning disability grouping. *Transact. Anal. J.*, 1971, 1, 209–213.

Ernst, K. *Games students play*. Millbrae, Calif.: Celestial Arts Pub., 1972.

Everts, K. V. The president's page. *Transact. Anal. J.*, 1973, 3, 4.

Harris, T. A. *I'm OK — You're OK: a practical guide to transactional analysis*. New York: Harper & Row, 1967.

James, J. The game plan. *Transact. Anal. J.*, 1973, 3, 194–197.

James, M. & Jongeward, D. *Born to win: transactional analysis with Gestalt experiments*. Reading, Mass.: Addison-Wesley Pub. Co., 1971.

————. *Winning with people. Group exercises in transactional analysis.* Reading, Mass.: Addison-Wesley Pub. Co., 1973.

Karpman, S. B. Fairytales and script drama analysis. *Transact. Anal. Bull.*, 1968, 7, 39–43.

————. Developments in transactional analysis. *Current Psychiatric Ther.*, 1972, 12, 132–150.

Kelly, G. A. Looks who's talking — a review of transactional analysis in psychotherapy. *Contemp. Psychol.*, 1963, 8, 189–190.

Kupfer, D. & Haimowitz, M. Therapeutic interventions. Part I. Rubberbands now. *Transact. Anal. J.*, 1971, 1, 10–16.

Maslow, A. H. *Motivation and personality*. New York: Harper & Row, 1954.

Miller, A. B. & Maloney, D. Turn-over. *Transact. Anal. J.*, 1972, 2, 117–121.

Nelson, R. C. *Guidance and counseling in the elementary school*. New York: Holt, Rinehart & Winston, Inc., 1972.

Orten, J. Contributions to stroke vocabulary. *Transact. Anal. J.*, 1972, 2, 104–106.

Penfield, W. Memory mechanisms. A.M.A. *Arch. Neurol. & Psychiat.*, 1952, 67, 178–198.

Shapiro, S. B. Critique of Eric Berne's contributions to subself theory. *Psychol. Reports.*, 1969, 25, 283–296.

Steiner, C. Script and counterscript. *Transact. Anal. Bull.*, 1966, 5, 133–135.

Thamm, R. Self-acceptance and acceptance of others: exploration into personality syndromes. *Transact. Anal. J.*, 1972, 2, 139–147.

INDEX

Abbey, D. S., 74
Activities, 17, 32
Adult ego states, 2, 9, 12–13
  contaminated, 13, 33–34, 48
  defined, 10, 12
  function of, 10, 12
Allen, J. G., 51, 75
Archaepsyche, 11
Berne, E., 1, 3–15, 17–30, 32–35, 38–40,
    42–46, 48–50, 53, 56, 63, 65–67,
    73, 75
Campos, L. P., 73
Cathexis, 14, 45
Cheney, W. D., 6–8, 75
Child ego state, 2, 6, 9–11, 13
  Adapted Child, 13
  defined, 10, 13
  function of, 10, 13
  Natural Child, 13
Communication, nature of, 5
Contamination, 13, 33–34, 48
Counseling
  and game analysis, 63
  and structural analysis, 53–54
  and transactional analysis, 54–55,
    66–67
  groups, 63
Counselor
  accountability, 68–69
  and student-teacher relationships,
    55–56
  assistance in stopping games, 61–64
  role in transactional analysis, 55
Counterscript, 24
Decommissioned ego states, 13, 34
Decontamination, 45, 48
Diagnosis of ego states, 43–44
Diagnostic categories, 4–5
Dusay, J. M., 5, 75
Ego states, 1, 6, 9–11, 13, 36, 37
  cathexis of, 14
  contamination of, 13, 33–34

decommissioned, 13, 34
definition of, 9
English, F., 10, 75
Erikson, E., 3
Ernst, F. H., Jr., 67, 76
Ernst, J. L., 66, 76
Ernst, K., 56–60, 62–63, 73, 76
Everts, K. V., 7, 76
Exteropsyche, 11
Facial expressions, 43
Feelings Rackets, 21, 31, 65
Freed, A., 74
Fromm-Reichmann, F., 4
Freud, S., 10
Game Plan, 61
Games, 2, 33, 47
  analysis as technique, 42
  analysis of, 2, 17–20, 56–60
  definition of, 2, 9, 17
  in therapy, 39–40
  Karpman formula, 20
  student, 56–60
  teacher, 60
Groups, 38–40
  counseling, 63
  parent and teacher, 68–69
  preparation for, 38
  research in, 38
  size, 39
Haimowitz, M., 46, 76
Harris, T. A., 4, 27–29, 32–33, 74, 76
International Transactional Analysis As-
    sociation, 4, 7
  membership categories, 50
  standards for training, 50
Intervention techniques, 44–46
Intimacy, 17, 33
Intuition
  and child, 5
  definition of, 4
  studies, 4–6
James, M., 23, 29, 46, 61, 65, 74, 76

77

"Discount Transaction," 41
"Gallows Transaction," 41
ulterior, 5, 17, 55
Vocabulary
  of ego states, 12, 44
  of Transactional Analysis, 2, 14, 37

Vocal signals, 43–44
Voices in the Head, 48–49
Withdrawal, 17, 32